The 66 Rules of Greatness:
A Practical Guide to Your Personal Development.

Ejayeta Jay Ipheghe

© Copyright 2015 by Ejayeta Jay Ipheghe

Published in Nigeria by
Expression Hour
2nd Avenue 206 Road,
B Close, House 8,
Festac Town Lagos

ISBN: 978-978-945-763-2

All rights reserved. No part of this publication may be reproduced, stored in a retrieval system, or transmitted in any form or by any means; electronic, mechanical, photocopying, recording or otherwise, without the prior written permission of the copyright owner. The only exception is brief quotation in print or electronic reviews.

Set at 11pt Book Antiqua
In Microsoft Word 2007 by University of Port Harcourt Printing Press Ltd

DEDICATION

To my wonderful dad and mum-
Barrister Gabriel I. Ipheghe and Queen Ipheghe

ACKNOWLEDGEMENTS

My deepest appreciation goes to God-Almighty. You are always there for me and you always see me through.

My profound regard goes to my dad and mum: Barr. G. I. Ipheghe and Mrs Queen Ipheghe. I truly appreciate the fact that you have always wanted the best for me. Thank you for your priceless investment on me. Special thanks to my brothers and sisters also.

Special thanks to Dandison Abbey, for your constructive advices, and the University of Port Harcourt Press for the very wonderful formatting and book cover design.

Thanks to many others.

E. J. Ipheghe

TABLE OF CONTENT

Dedication --- iii
Acknowledgements -- iv
Introduction -- 1
Source of greatness -- 1
Rules -- 1
Action -- 2
Time --- 2

(1) Man Enters The World With Closed Hands, As If to Say "The World is Mine" He leaves it With Open Hands As If to Say; "Behold I take Nothing With Me."
- The Midrash (AD 400-500) ---------------------------------- 3

(2) What We Need Are More People Who Specialize in The Impossible.
-Theodore Roethke. -- 9

(3) To Be Conscious That You Are Ignorant is a Great Step to Knowledge.
-Benjamin Disreali (1804-81) --------------------------------- 11

(4) The First Step in The Acquisition of Wisdom is Silence, The Second Listening, The Third, Memory, The Fourth, Practice, The Fifth Teaching Others.
-Solomon Gabriel --- 15

(5) I Have Gained This by Philosophy That I Do Without Being Commanded What Others Do Only From Fear of The Law
- Aristotle (384-322BC) --------------------------------------- 19

(6) Making Your Mark on The World is Hard. If It Were Easy, Everybody Would Do it; But It's not. It Takes Patience, It Takes Commitment, and It Comes With Plenty of Failure Along The Way.
- Barrack Obama -- 21

(7) A Real Decision is Measured By The Fact That You've Taken a New Action. If There's No Action, You Have Not Truly Decided.
- Tony Robins -- 25

(8) Often The Difference Between a Successful Man and a Failure is Not One's Better Abilities or Ideas, But The Courage That One Has to Bet on His Ideas, To Take a Calculated Risk, and to Act.
- Maxwell Mattz -- 29

(9) There is No Reason to Cry in Pains. Just look into yourself and Appreciate What You've Got and Happiness Would Come Your Way. ---------------------- 33

(10) It's Easy to Break a Broom Stick But Impossible to Break its Bunch. That Proves That Unity is Strength.-----------37

(11) Your Life is Like a Rent, One Day You're Going to Evacuate it and Give an Account of How You Lived it. Do Not Ever Forget This While on Earth. ---------------- 41

(12) It Takes Two to Fall in Love or Else It Becomes a Dangerous Affair.-- 47

(13) Be Careful of The Kind and Type of Seed That You Sow Because It Will Also Determine The Kind and Type of Harvest You Shall Reap. ------------------------------------ 53

(14) If You Have Dream Without Problems, Then You Don't Really Have a Dream
- John Mason --- 57

(15) We Make a Living By What We Get, But We Make A Life By What We Give.
- Norman Macewan -- 61

16)   A Successful Man Is One Who Can Lay A Firm Foundation With The Bricks That Others Throw At Him
- John Mason --- 63

(17) It Only Takes A Small Courage To Start, But A Big Daily Dose Of It To Keep Going, Because You'll Feel Like quitting A Thousand Times Before You Get To The Top
- Bob Gass-- 67

(18) The Rich Man Has A Language… So Also Is the Poor Man-- 71

(19) When You Try To Spend Less, You End Up Spending More-- 75

(20) Presence of love in our hearts makes us angels but lack of it turns us into monsters-------------------------------------- 77

(21) Revenge makes you put more burdens on yourself than the actual one being put on you by another person.-----79

(22) Become an Authority on Something
- John Mason --- 83

(23) In life, there's no such thing as calculated risk because risk is risk; nothing less. ------------------------------------- 85

(24) When chasing your dreams, go for the standard your heart desires and do not ever try to compromise. ------ 87

(25) In whatever chosen field of career that you find yourself, be a professional so you can grow. ------------ 89

(26) There Is More Vision Extinguisher Than Vision Molders -- 91

(27) God has given to us a minimum of one talent but the capacity to manage it properly does not always rest with us and that's why you need to look for your manger today.---------------------- -------------------------------------- 95

(28) Heaven helps those who help themselves. Unknown --- 99

(29) The little things one does are what make the difference as long as you are consistent. -----------------------------103

(30) There is no problem that builds in a day. The day you noticed it is the day that it got matured meaning that it has been developing for a while. -------------------------107

(31) What happens to you doesn't matter. How you handle the situations that you find yourself is what matters-109

32) Disappointments, Regrets, Betrayals Are Part of Life's Ingredient That Helps In Preparing Us to Be Done---113

(33) There Is No Problem That Will Come To You Without The Ability You Need To Solve It As Well.--------------117

(34) God Has Given Man The Ability To See The Visions Ahead But Not The Circumstances That Will Prepare Him For Its Actualization. ---------------------------------119

(35) Man Planeth But God Decides. ----------------------------123

(36) "God is God"---127

(37) Big Income Doesn't Make One Rich But How You Control Your Expenditure Do.-----------------------------131

(38) Only Trust Those That Sees The Sorrow Behind Your Smile, The Love Behind Your Anger And The Reason Behind Your Silence. --135

(39) If You Do Not Believe In Yourself First, Nobody Else Will Believe In You Either.---------------------------------137

(40) When Setting Up An Enterprise, Spend More Time To Draft Your Vision And Mission Statement Because They Are The Most Important. ----------------------------------141

(41) Circumstances Are The Rulers Of The Weak; But They Are The Instrument Of The Wise.
- Samuel Glover ---145

(42) There Is No Moment Like The Present. The Man Who Will Not Execute His Resolution When They Are Fresh On Him Can Have No Hope From Them Afterward; For They Will Be Dissipated Lost, And Perished In The Hung And Scurry Of The World Or Sunk In The Slough Of Indolence.
- John Buroughs --149

(43) What I Gave, I Have
What I Spent, I Had
What I Kept, I Lost.
- Old Epitaph -- 153

(44) No Man Could Be Ideally Successful Until He Has Found His Place. Like a Locomotive, He Is Strong On Track, But Weak Anywhere Else
-Orison Marden--- 157

(45) Don't Relax, Keep On Breaking Your Record and Setting a New One--- 161

(46) The Best Investment So Far, So Good Is The One On Human Being -- 165

(47) We Are All Something but None of Us Is Everything-169

(48) You Can Only Make It By His Grace ---------------------- 171

(49) The More You Grow, The More Clean Your Hands Should Become --- 175

(50) Always Forgive Those That Trespass Against You --- 177

(51) I Have Found Out That If You Love Life, Life Will Love You Back
-Arthur Rubinstein --------------------------------------- 181

(52) The Greatest Pleasure of Life Is Love
- Euripides --- 183

(53) In Every Situation, Recognize Who The Boss Is. -------- 185

(54) Play Loyalty -- 189

(55) Influence Directly or Indirectly, Which Ever Ways, Make Sure You Are Influencing. ------------------------- 193

(56) Running Too Fast Does Not Guarantee That You Will Get To Your Destination. ------------------------------------ 197

(57) Enter Action with Boldness --------------------------------- 201

(58) The Crowd Is Foolish but the Individual Is Wise ------ 207

(59) Be Grateful For Your Yesterday, Today and the Future --- 211

(60) Make Your Expectations Moderate. -------------------------- 215

(61) Your Decisions of Yesterday Made Your Today And Your Decisions of Today Would Make Your Tomorrow --- 219

(62) No Trumpet Sound When the Important Decision of Our Life Are Made. Destiny Is Made Known Silently --- 223

(63) Everybody Has Their Own Definition of Success But One Thing Is Sure: Success Is A Positive Growth In Any Aspect Of Our Lives --------------------------------------- 227

(64) The Road To Success Is Full Of Stress So If You Must Succeed, You Must Learn How To Manage Stress ---- 229

(65) Life And Death Is In The Tongue, Be Careful Of The One You Let Out --- 233

(66) We Have Dreams and Destiny But Our Destiny Supersedes Our Dreams------------------------------------237

Index-- --241

INTRODUCTION

Source of Greatness

Greatness comes from God Almighty. He is the one that created the earth and everything in it. The purpose for our living is destiny. He was the one who carved our destiny as well. Through the fulfillment of our destiny, we become great. The moment you are unable to fulfill your destiny, you are far from being great. So you must do everything to seek God's face so you can at least have an idea of the path you are supposed to follow.

Rules

Everything in this life is governed by rules. Just name it and I will tell you it's rules. To be great equally has its rules. Rules can be further divided into two main category-General and specific.

General rules are those rules that apply to the achievement of a broad goal. You must be ok with the general rules before you can proceed because it serves as the foundation upon which other rules are based.

Specific rules are those rules that you need to follow to get little assignments done. The achievement of these little assignments is what leads to overall success of the set goals and objectives.

One general rule to greatness anywhere in the world is hard work. There is no substitute. If your goal were to be in the area of academic, a specific rule is "reading".

Action

Greatness is the reward gotten from series upon series of right actions. Your actions has to be right as well.

Time

This is another very important factor to being great. It is not a day job. Do not try to build Rome in a day. After all, nothing good comes easy. Each day comes with its job. Just be consistent by always doing each day's job and at the appointed time, you will achieve it.

I do really wish you a happy reading and please do us a favor: apply the principles and guidelines suggested in this book and you will forever be glad that you did. If we are all great, it would be a very big plus to humanity.

CHAPTER 1

Man Enters the World with Closed Hands, as If to Say "The world is mine" He Leaves it With Open Hands as If to Say; "Behold I Take Nothing With Me."
— The Midrash (AD 400-500)

This is to say that no one was born by accident; because being born with closed hands signifies that there is something special you have come into the world with. The hands are closed because you have to protect that thing – that special gift deposited in you by God.

Let us now assume the hands were opened, it could have been very possible for another person to just come and take away that talent. That means we have a duty-the duty of protecting what we have unless it will be stolen. No wonder God said in the bible "the thief cometh in the night but to kill and steal".

Again there is no newly born baby with hands opened meaning every child comes with his or her special gift. It is possible that your parents gave birth to you when they were not legally married, or when you were born, your dad rejected you. There are even cases where by the child is abandoned by both parents –the mother and the father but whichever the case might be, but for the fact that you are still alive up to this moment, that shows that you have a purpose in life to fulfill. Do not ever leave the world without fulfilling that purpose.

Let us assume you have been destined to be a medical doctor, a surgeon or what's more a nurse and then life became harsh for you to bear or somehow you gave up your dreams and couldn't become the medical doctor. Already God who made you has gone ahead to create up to about 10,000 children who will be sick at one period of a time or another for you to rescue. So tell me what's going to be the fate of these children? If you do not become the doctor, of course you and I know they will perish and they are not just perishing on their own but you made them perish because you refused to fulfill your purpose. A lot of us believe we have never killed before but unknown to us that we have killed many times simply by not being there at the right time to save a life. Do you know that a single word in a song can prevent someone from committing suicide? What if the artiste had not sang the song before then?

One thing we should all know is that, at every single time we do not fulfill our purpose in life, there is bound to be problem somewhere.

The special thing in you can be anything. It could be the gift of writing, speaking, singing, studying etc. The most important thing is that you utilize that gift in order to improve human kind.

A man leaves the world with hands opened which signifies that he has given us all that he had to offer to improve human kind and now I am going back with none. But it is also possible that he didn't even fulfill his purpose but he is going back with hands opened just like every other human being that once lived. There are so many demonic spirits all around the world. They are around the world. They are around to steal and to kill and to destroy. So it is either you fulfill your purpose or you waste it but what you should know is that you are leaving the world without it.

So now your duties are:
Find your purpose in life.
Preserving the purpose and
Utilizing the purpose.

We shall state the above steps one after the other starting from step one.

Finding Out Your Purpose
"Purpose", according to the Oxford advanced learners dictionary means "the intention, aim or function of something. It refers to the goal a particular thing is supposed to achieve. By this definition, you will agree with me that purpose refers to the reason why a human is being born into the world. So first of all in order to discover your purpose, look into yourself, try to pick out that thing you love doing the most-that natural gift of yours that you didn't have to learn how to do. For instance, you find yourself singing all the time and whenever you do it, it brings fulfillment to you. You can call it natural medicine.

Trace yourself down to your childhood, what were the things you love the most or things you find yourself doing whenever you are free. Did you like argument so much? Your true call might be to be a lawyer or a speaker. I know this may be hard for you because it is possible to like more than two things but then try hard to see how they relate. For instance you may be faced with being a pastor and at the same time a singer. The best way to handle it is by linking both talents. Through your songs, you can preach the gospel. And don't forget to always ask God for guidance. He gave you the talent and He is in the best position to show you the appropriate way to use it.

Preserving the Purpose
Now that you have known your purpose, your duty is to preserve it. Make sure it is alive every day. Don't ever let it die,

but rather, let it shine so everyone could see it and you'll become a source of inspiration to others who are watching you. Always have it in your mind, "there is always somebody watching you; you may never know"

I have seen many instances where people abandon their true call for another call with the hope of coming back someday to their true call but never returned.

They say practice makes perfect and that's true. Your talent is in a raw form; it needs refining and the best way to refine it is to start using it and over a period of time you will discover how well you've come. But let's assume you left it, it will either remain how you left it or it must have depreciated. And again do not forget to ask God for the strength to proceed because it is neither by your power nor by your might.

Utilize the Purpose
It is true that what you have is your talent but somehow it is not yours because you are not the reason why it was given to you. It was given to you to become a source of blessings to the needing and source of hope to the depressed so the only way you can say you are utilizing your purpose, it is when you start using it to touch lives.

For instance, the stars in the sky shines into the world but they starts to die the moment they shine into themselves. It simply means that you are not living for yourself. Nelson Mandela did not fight for freedom for himself neither did Martin-Luther King fight against racism for himself alone. Always look forward to what you can give and not what you can receive from the world. Until then, the world would not become a better place for me and you.

Still talking about how to utilize your purpose, the only way is when you use it to touch lives.

You have been blessed with something very special; find it out and use it to contribute your quota into the world. By the time we all do this, the world would become a better place for me and you.

CHAPTER 2

What We Need Are More People Who Specialize in The Impossible.
-Theodore Roethke.

The two key words here are "specialize" and "the impossible".
To start with, what does it mean to specialize? According to Oxford Advance Learner Dictionary, to "specialize" means to become an expert in a particular area of work or study or business; to spend more time on one area of work etc than on others while "impossible" that cannot exist or be done; not possible or something that is very difficult to deal with. From the definition of these two words we can say that specialization in the impossible means doing or achieving the extra ordinary or what people had thought is hard to achieve. Now, the quote above is telling you that we need such people of extra-ordinary bravery, who will go against the odds to do what people had thought would be impossible.

A man named Barrack Obama who is black became the first African-American president of the United States of America. Before then, people had thought it to be impossible. This man worked hard, stood against many obstacles in his way; they did not discourage him but made him stronger. It is even possible that a lot of people including friends and families must have told him he was wasting his time but he did not allow all that to kill his dream; he held on to his dream of becoming a president in the country that is so great.

It took time, it took a lot of energy and a lot of planning but the good news is that: At last he got what he was looking for. Or is it Martin Luther-king? He was another great fighter who fought against the discrimination against African-Americans in America. It was his dream that one day, an African-American man would become an American president and though he did not live to see this happened but his dream eventually came to pass when Mr. Barrack Obama became the first African-American U.S president. To tell you the truth, it is not easy but that doesn't mean it is impossible.

CHAPTER 3

To Be Conscious That You Are Ignorant is a Great Step to Knowledge.
              -Benjamin Disreali (1804-81)

When you do not know and you don't know that you do not know, how are you going to start knowing? There is no worst degree of ignorance than this because if you don't know that you do not know, you can't even make changes.

I used to have one friend then in school, when you are talking or explaining something to him; he doesn't let you land, the next thing you will hear from him is: "I know". But the truth still remain that he doesn't know. I call that a problem and it may be as a result of pride or something else but this attitude has rubbed him of a lot of things. I mean a lot of blessing that he could have gotten by just mere listening. My friend is not the only person with this kind of attitude. A lot of people are too; both in low, average and high places. I can tell of so many politicians who never listened to the voice of the people they were suppose to serve and eventually they had to obey the law of gravity in such an unceremonious way. They thought they know it all but didn't.

No matter how small or lowly placed a man may be, learn to always listen to people. The truth is "you can learn from anybody". You may be a professor in Harvard or Oxford University, it doesn't stop you from learning from the peasant farmer or gardener and he or she can as well learn from you. That is to say knowledge is no respecter of a man's status. Just as death is no respecter of a man's status also.

This problem of one not knowing and they don't know that they don't know is caused by pride most of the time. The pride being referred to here is not that type that people usually feel about their country, people or things they value so much but the "feeling that you are better or more important than other people" and as a result feels too big to listen or interact with others.

At the first place, I cannot even understand why some human beings should feel too pompous to listen to their fellow human-being speaking to them. After all, we are all created by one God and God has deposited different gifts in us with each person specializing in a particular area.

Now let us imagine a case whereby one does not know and he knows that he does not know. Such a person knowing very well that he does not know would start longing to know and when someone talks to him, he listens so he can know better.

Solomon in the bible took after his father-David as the king of Israel. First, he wasn't even the father's first born and secondly, his mother was not even a hundred percent legitimate wife to David but her son Solomon took after the father as the new king of Israel.

Solomon in his time was the wisest man on earth. The bible says that he asked God for wisdom. He did not ask for wealth neither did he asked for fame. All he asked for was wisdom and every other thing followed. First he was aware he did not know and secondly he was humble enough to request from God.

Zacchaeus in the bible was a very wealthy tax collector. He wanted to be born again but didn't know how. Even when his height wouldn't allow him to see Jesus, he had to climb a tree. That was a display of awareness that he doesn't know and humility made him to seek knowledge and at the end, the truth was revealed to him.

The world is so beautiful that God made no man to be an Island likewise no nation to be an Island. You must depend on the other person for one thing or the other that you do not have. Nations depend upon nation if not, there wouldn't have been anything like international trade but thank God, what I have, you don't have and what you have, I don't have and nature have it that I must need the other things I do not have so I must exchange with the other person that has what I am looking for or better still call it sharing and they say, there is love in sharing.

Sometimes people know that they do not know but still, they find it hard to make enquiries because of one thing-their nature. Your nature could be extrovert or an introvert. I will take my time here to explain these two concepts but we are going to dwell more on introvert but first.

Extrovert
This is that someone who is very lively. This is the life of every party or social gathering. It could be a friend birthday party or friends get together, any gathering at all. The moment he shows up, the party gets started. He is also very confidential person that enjoys being with other people. This kind of person always look forward to meeting people and as a result of this kind of nature, he can easily penetrate into anywhere. If he doesn't know anything or much about a thing, he can easily meet people who have and consult them. This makes him to know a lot. Remember I told you he enjoys meeting people and also like to attend socials; what this implies is that he will know a lot and will probably continue to know more as he continue to be with or meet other people.

Introvert

An introvert is a highly reserved person. This kind of person doesn't really like to be in the limelight. They are usually very quiet and they do all the thinking by themselves. This is because naturally they do not like to mingle and if you do not like to mingle, how are you going to trust some other person enough to ask him or her questions about a particular thing you do not understand or how are you going to even share your problems with another person. Most people like that usually die in silence. It is one thing to know that you don't know and it is another thing for you to be able to contact those who can help you. The problem might not be pride but the nature of this type of people to always keep to themselves.

There are some feature that, we, humans have naturally. Some, we can change and some others, we can do nothing about. But the ones we can change, let's try our best to change them. If you find it hard to approach people, try to kill whatever spirit that may be responsible for that. Even though you are naturally a very reserved person, try as much as possible to come out of that sometimes. Life is all about trying to strike the balance. To tell you the truth, many entertainers we have today couldn't face the crowd before. Michael Jackson, one of the world's greatest entertainer that ever lived was also an introvert. Try to find out this by yourself, the story of many of the best musicians, movie stars and other TV personalities the world has produced; most did badly in their first appearance. What I want you to know is that you can always make changes; if not totally, but, at least to some extent. Imagine a world whereby no one feels he or she knows it all.

CHAPTER 4

The First Step in the Acquisition of Wisdom is Silence, The Second Listening, The Third, Memory, The Fourth, Practice, The Fifth Teaching Others.

- Solomon Gabriel

Silence in the context above is not a noun but a verb so it is an act. Before we go further, lets discuss the main thing "wisdom". In your own view, what is wisdom? Many people will come out with different definitions but the fact remains that wisdom is a good thing and everyone wants to have it.

According to the Oxford Advance Learners Dictionary, wisdom is the ability to make reasonable decisions and give good advice because of experience and knowledge that you have. By following this definition, we can say that wisdom is as a result of lessons learned from past mistakes.

In a nutshell, wisdom is that substance which enable you to make reasonable decision; decisions that are powerful or decision that can hardly be regretted. Whenever you've been through a situation and that situation presents itself again; based on your previous encounter, you would be able to deal with it more successfully.

The wisest men and women the world has ever produced are known to be slow talkers. They spend most of their time in keeping silence while they think or listen. They never rushed to make decisions. In fact most decision made in haste always yields more problems and as a result pain and regret. You can try to look back and remember some of your most regrettable decisions, they were made in haste. Imagine the story of Solomon in the bible when two women who were dragging for the ownership of a baby was brought to him, while the two women present their cases, King Solomon kept silent and was slow to speak. The woman who wasn't the mother of the baby agreed that the baby should be divided into two half for them to share. Immediately, the true owner of the child started to weep. At that point Solomon was able to save the baby and gave it to the true owner. This is to tell you that silence and listening are very good steps to getting wisdom.

The next step is memory. Memory is the ability to remember things or events. It is the part of the human that is responsible for storing information. Picture of events that had already taken place are recorded in the brain also. Any man who can remember up to half of the things that he reads would be the most brilliant person on earth. The ability to remember things quickly is the edge a brilliant student has over the non-brilliant one.

I always tell people that no one is born dull. It all depends on your ability to strain the brain and the ability to remember. This accounts for the reason why students are always advice to read. One thing is to read, and the other is having a space in your brain to store the information that you have got.

Also there are some kinds of foods that can enhance the human brain. Such foods like egg, fish, fruits and so on or better still consult your nearest doctor; ask him to give you list of foods that can boost your remembering ability. The memory is very important for so many reasons. One of it is that it serves as an information warehouse of the human system. Lets assume you are a business man who is into buying and selling of perishable goods; you have a warehouse but it is filled up already but you are done for the day's business whereas you still have some goods left, tell me what do you think would happen to the remaining goods if not properly preserve? Of course they would perish. When you keep learning and studying, you prevent the brain from redundancy.

Another step to the acquisition of wisdom is **practice**. This simply means action not ideas. Already you have the ideal, now is time to put it to practice. There is a popular saying that goes "practice makes perfect". Something you learnt today, if you continue to do it over and all over again, you'll find out that it becomes part of you and any day you do not do it, you feel like you are not yourself.

Michael Jordan is good in basket ball. Yes! We know but that wasn't enough for him to become world best; it was series of practices he made. In fact, he isn't the only one good at the ball; a lot of them are but his name rings more bells because he probably practiced harder. Let us talk about David Beckham, he is uniquely different from other foot ball players because of the extra time he devoted to practicing.

Knowing something or having something is not enough to bring out the best in us but constant practice. Anything we know or have may rust or decay over time but constant practice is like the refinery that refines it. This is just like mineral deposits in a country. They need to be refined before they can be used.

The final but not the least is "**teaching others**". I'm sure you'll be wondering what concerns others with what you know. There are some students who read all the time. Whichever information they have obtained, they always want to keep it to themselves. They don't like sharing. They always want to keep it to themselves so that they alone, will know it. But at the end, the best they come out with is average grades.

The universe has a plan. Its own very plan is different from that of a human. I remember then, when I first started to learn about computers, my teacher said that the computer system is like garbage in, garbage out. What it means is that whatever you give to the computer, it gives back to you. That's exactly how the universe is. Whatever you sow, you reap or have you seen a farmer who sowed beans and ripped rice? No! They say one good tongue deserves another. The truth is whatever you give, you get.

People who learn something, and after knowing it, they teach other people never really forget that thing again. When you know something and you teach another person, it is like insuring what you know, you will discover that you will never really forget that thing again.

I have a friend back then in school, he used to teach me mathematics. In the process of teaching me, he makes mistakes and then when we get to the final answer, we will find out that the answer does not correspond and then we will go back again to solving in order to locate where the problem is. You will agree with me that the mistakes he made during the teaching would have been the ones he could have made in the examination hall but for the fact that he already made mistakes while teaching me, he wrote very well. So you can see how "this law operates". He taught me and then universe taught him even better.

So in conclusion, in acquisition of wisdom, these five major steps below must be taken into consideration.
- **Silence**
- **Listening**
- **Memory**
- **Practices**
- **Teaching others**

You must follow it in this sequence.

CHAPTER 5

I Have Gained This by Philosophy That I Do Without Being Commanded What Others Do Only From Fear of the Law
Aristotle (384-322BC)

The name Aristotle is not a very common name that people bear but in almost all history books, you may find the name there. They all talk about one particular Aristotle. He was a great philosopher. In fact, there is no way you can escape reading about this man as a scholar irrespective of the field of study you belong to.

Here, Aristotle tells you that he has gained this by philosophy meaning this had become part of him. What has become part of him? He goes on to explain that he does things he believes are right to do not because he will be punished for not doing them.

You know that in every society, there are norms, culture, morals, custom and a particular way of life. Any behavior that is contrary to these norms or custom of the society is being seen as a deviant behavior; something that is considered to be wrong and unacceptable.

There are people who don't just do the right thing willingly. The only time they do something right is because of fear of being punished by the law. Let us assume there are no laws, rules and regulations, these set of people would turned into nuisance because there is nothing good they would willingly do in the society. These sets of people are life parasites in the society. They are societal liabilities to the society in which they live in because when others are building, they are breaking. They are not addition but minus to the society. This is not good at all.

Aristotle tries to make us understand that if we do the right thing without being threatened by the law, our society would become a better place. We are humans and as humans, we are higher than the animals. God has given to us the sense needed to differentiate bad from good. Let us use it wisely. As a human, you have conscience, and that means we know which is bad and which is good. Why don't we make it a habit to always do the good thing or else how can we make the world a better place? How can we show the next generation the good path to follow? These are the question we should be asking ourselves.

Before you do anything at all, think about your society, think about your generations unborn and think about you. There is no way you do something to yourself without it affecting some other person. That is to tell you that this world is not only about you so always think of others before you do anything.

There are so many reasons or circumstances responsible for this kind of behavior. I believe there is no human that is born a liability. So many people today do the things they do because of frustration. It could also be lack of home training or as a way of disposing their dissatisfaction against the state. Whichever reason it may be, the point still remain that no one has any excuses to be bad. If you say, the society is bad, but what about the other people who are making it without breaking the law. If we start to give reasons for being bad, everybody in the society would be bad.

CHAPTER 6

Making Your Mark on the World is Hard. If It Were Easy, Everybody would do it; but It's not. It Takes Patience, It Takes Commitment, and It Comes With Plenty of Failure Along The Way.
- Barrack Obama

It is hard to make your mark on the world. It is hard to come out great and it is also very hard to make history that generations after generation would read or hear about. Indeed it is hard but it is also good that way. VIP (very important personality) is not for everyone. Usually the crown is for one person. It is not everyone that will be president. No. but it is good this way. Don't you think so? At least let there be a master and at the same time a servant. How hard you've worked determines your placement in the society. So it is left for you to decide where you would like to be and work accordingly.

Human beings have dreams. Anyone who does not have dreams isn't living. We are all dreamers. So now, the issue is not about whether you dream but it is about how big your dream is and how hard you are willing to work to get there. Although to make your mark on the world is hard, I still advice you to dream big. You should dream big as much as you can. You should dream beyond the stars and the moon in the sky so at most you'll fall within the stars and moon.

To make a mark on the world has to be hard so that only the strong ones can be at the top. I know that you need also be very smart but you still need hard work. It is this level of hard work that determines our speed and how close we are getting to our dreams. Also remember "it is not how long but how well". Some people achieve what took others ten years to achieve in just five years. A typical example of this is the entertainment industry. This is where you see an upcoming artiste who is far better than some old artistes and within a short time the new artiste becomes bigger than his seniors.

Let us take a view of the university system whereby the sheep is separated from the goat by grading. There are the A materials and there are also the B or C materials down to the F materials so if you are a "C" material for instance, you want to upgrade to "B", you know the amount of hard work to add up.

Anyone who wants to be great wants to make history, anything at all you want to become, may be to be the best in your field of study, just anything at all, know that you must embrace hard work. Pay this price and you will be fulfilled when you get it. Let us make hard work our way of life.

To make a mark on the world also takes **patience**. First you will have to work hard and secondly, you need patience. No matter how hard you have worked, your harvest might not be immediate. In fact great harvests have never been immediate. They say that "Rome was not built in a day" what this means is that it is the series of works and decisions you make today that determines your tomorrow. The biggest business enterprises today were some few years back very small. Talk about the shopping wall-mart. They had to start from somewhere. When you see a sky scraper, you admire it but remember it wasn't built in a day. Just keep working, keep sowing and one day your seeds will mature.

The ant is a very tiny animal but it knows how to gather food during dry season to store and during raining season, sits back to enjoy. Because it has worked enough during the dry season, now that it is raining season, the ants sit back to enjoy the fruit of his labor. Take your time one day to study the ant, you will find out that all they do is to carry bits of food such as sugar into their hole because that is where their house is and during raining season, they don't bother about coming out because they have gathered enough to eat. If small creatures like that could be so organized, what about us-the so called higher animals or you preferred to be called a human. Think about it and decide.

Another very important step is **commitment**. To be committed means simply to believe in something and to willingly decide to work hard and give your time to it.

Let us assume that by now, you have a dream, that is, something you would like to become later in the future and you've been working hard towards achieving this dream. Now the role of commitment here is your belief that you will become that thing. Although you are still working towards it but already you see a mental picture of yourself being that thing. This is to tell you that commitment can be a way of expressing your faith or hope. This is what you need if you dream to become the best graduating student of your set, let it be that already, you see a mental picture of yourself being celebrated that way.

May be you want to be a famous and a sensational singer; try to carve a picture in your mind when you've already become that star.

To tell you the truth, I so much love music and everything about me is music. Music is my life and almost everything. Since I was ten years old, I have been looking forward to a successful career in music. I am not yet that star, I mean not yet the famous and well respected singer I want to be but I already have a mental picture on my mind whereby I sing on stage and the crowd is really feeling me. I have this picture of me signing autograph, and paparazzi chasing me and so much more. When you already see yourself achieving the dream, it will make you to remain focus.

We cannot deny the fact that there are always obstacles. Don't worry, they will make you stronger. There has to be obstacles in your way in order to bring out the best in you. You know the way it happens in schools. You will have to write examinations before you are promoted to next level of class. If you passed very well, it is a way of knowing if you can cope in the next level or not. So when you see obstacles do not panic or be depressed but instead, see it as an opportunity to cross to the next level.

At this point, your mindset matters a whole lot, focus your mind on success not failure or else you will surely get the failure. Be careful of what you think because it might just happen. Think success always even when you fail, try to find out the cause of your failure and re-plan because if truly practice makes perfect, then as you keep trying, one day you will become perfect and hit the right spot.

One beautiful thing is that how many times you fail doesn't matter but if you win at the end. Have you noticed, when people suddenly make it and began to live well, we easily forget about their past. I mean how unhealthy they used to look. One thing you should note is that your win serves as a payback for your failures.

Ben Carson, the renowned surgeon wasn't bright at all in school and the other students usually make jest of him. But the moment he started reading hard, he became very bright and now how many people can still remember how dull he used to be.

The good news is that when you win, people must celebrate you, so focus on your winning and never mind how many times you have failed.

CHAPTER 7

A Real Decision is measured by the Fact That You've Taken a New Action. If there's No Action, You Have Not Truly Decided.

- Tony Robins

Anything that is good always has a bad side also just like we have, "anything that is original must have its fake also. But Tony Robins is not concerned about you making decisions. What he is concerned about is the quality of your decision. How real or how original it is.

There is no person that doesn't make decision. In fact every day we make decisions. The time you woke up was a decision. The food you ate was a decision. This book you are reading now is a decision. Whether it is a condition that you like or don't like, it is as a result of your decision. Somebody could have put you in a place but it was still your decision to allow it.

A lot of people always look for someone to blame whenever they lost. They say it is that person that made them fail. They will now begin to point fingers at other people. But when they are successful, they will say "I made it" or like Jay-Z would say "I came, I saw and I Conquered". Now that you've made it, it is you that conquered. So when you fail also, you should take responsibility and try again.

As a man (humans), you should always learn to accept responsibilities whether bad or good. That's why you have to always try to do the right thing at all times and in case you miscalculate and the result comes out bad, accept it and go back to the drawing board.

We, humans cannot do without decision making. At every point in time we are faced with many options and we have to make a choice. We need to make the right decisions towards achieving the desired results. The following are important steps towards making good decisions.
- List out all you options.
- Write out each one of the options; its advantages and disadvantages.
- Find out from the option the one in which you have maximum resources to execute.
- Select the best option and follow up with action immediately.
- Be patient and very smart.

We shall discuss them one after the other in their sequence.

List out All Your Options
Anytime at all you are faced with the need to make a decision, there are always options. It is from these options that you will pick. In order not to make a wrong decision, list out all the options that you have.

Write Out Each Of The Options; Its Advantages And Disadvantages.
Lets assume you have three options, option A, B and C, it would be better for you to write out the advantages and disadvantages of option A. Do the same for option B and C in a tabular form.

Find Out From Among The Options The One In Which You Have Maximum Resources To Execute.
Through one way or the other you did economics while in school, you must have heard of comparative cost advantage under the topic of international trade. There, countries trading with other countries are being advised to concentrate in the production of goods that will be cheaper for them to produce more than any other country with the amount of resources they have. Which of the options do you have most resources; that with what you already have, you wouldn't need to sacrifice much? For instance, a country like Nigeria is naturally blessed with crude oil while another country may be more blessed in textile and animals; comparative cost advantage is saying that it would be cheaper for Nigeria to produce petrol than leather and she should focus more on that.

Select the best option and follow up with action immediately.
Already the best option had been selected in step 3. What we are looking out here is your follow up-action. A lot of time, we make decision but we don't follow it up with action. Later on we will now, find out that we never did what we decided. When we keep on like that, there is no difference between us and those who didn't plan at all? Do not leave a place of decision without an action. Let this be your habit. The moment you decide, lay the foundation even though you will do the rest later.

Be patient and very smart
You have to be patient and very smart because major sowings are not reaped in a day. On the other hand, be very smart because the moment you have decided, many forces would begin to act against your decision. So be prepared to stand against all odds in order to win.

One way to stand against all odds is to kill procrastination. Procrastination is the attitude of carrying actions forward to a future date. Anything you need to do now, just do it right away. There might never be next time because the more you delay, the more your time is getting tighter. You need to discipline yourself, know the time for play and the time for work.

Sometimes the kind of project may require a team work. Make sure you select people that share the same interest or similar view as you and also make sure they are competent. Team work is the best but when the team is not one, there is no worst scenario than it.

In conclusion, always make the right decision and followed it up with action because that is what differentiate you from a dreamer.

CHAPTER 8

Often The Difference Between a Successful Man and a Failure is Not One's Better Abilities or Ideas, But The Courage That One Has To Bet On His Ideas, To Take a Calculated Risk, and to Act.

Maxwell Mattz

When God created the universe, he put everything in it. Talk about wealth, talk about fame, talk about light, and talk about anything at all that is in this world, he created them all but gave them laws. These laws need to be interpreted and it takes one the courage that one has to bet on his ideas, to take a calculated risk and to act. The good news is that once you are able to decode the laws and obey them, you will surely get your desired result, but the problem of man is the courage to trust in his self or in his ideas.

When God created man (male and female), He also created everything that he will need. God is not like some men that will give birth to children into this world without planning for their arrival on earth. In fact, he created all that man would need before he even created man. You may go to the book of Genesis in the bible, which talks about recreation. There, you will find out that God created first, the stars, the moons, the sun, all that is in the sky and then created the trees, seas and ocean (all the water bodies), the atmosphere and all that is on earth. It was after all these things that He decided to create man-Adam.

To further convince you that God was truly after man's comfort, he created for him-Eve to be his company and helper. So now, if God can give Adam eve, another human who is just like him to be his company, what makes you feel that God has not given you even other things that you need also.

All you have to do is to put on your magnifying glasses. Put it on so you can see more clearly the opportunities around you. Man naturally is blind. Adam didn't know that he was naked until he ate of the tree of wisdom. Up till today man is still blind, to an extent. That's why you need a magnifying glass for you to be able to see clearly the potentials and powers in you. You need to know the kind of traits that you have and their importance. If not, how can you be able to utilize them? What is the difference between a man who has a land but doesn't know how to sow on it and a man who doesn't have a land to sow on?

By now, we must have all agreed that every man was born with his own abilities and ideas. These abilities are your instruments given to you by God to use to conquer the world. These instruments are hidden from the possessor. The possessor cannot see them unless he or she takes time to look for them. Now, it is time to search yourself, deep down into yourself, discover the strengths in you.

One thing I want you to know is that anybody you admire so much may be your hero but you were first, your own hero. Anything about you starts from you. When God bless you, it is on your seed. Anybody could have helped you but remember you helped yourself first.

Lets assume now that you have discover your ability. Remember Maxwell said that the difference between you and a failure is the courage that you have to be able to bet on your ability. This means that first, you need courage. So now how do you get this courage?

One thing is, knowing that you can do it and another thing again is trusting your capability to be able to do it. This is where you need courage. You will agree with me that you can never have the courage unless you've been practicing. Imagine a born singer. He knows he can sing but he has not been practicing or rehearsing, so how can he trust in his abilities. When will he be able to summon up the courage?

Until you practice or rehearse, you will never have the courage you need. Spend more time in development because it is the only way you can ensure or sharpens your instruments. When you have developed yourself, your confidence is restored and the courage that you need never goes away. This is the difference between you- a success and a failure.

As a man, if you don't have what you can die for, then you do not deserve to live. There must be something that you are connected with. It is your passion. Every human have their passion. If it is to be the president of your country, you should be ready to fight for it as long as you live. Do not settle for less. Martin Luther-king didn't settle for less; he fought all through his life time till he died. The man who truly fight for what he believes in, never really dies even if he is dead through assassination or by natural means. He goes as far as he can to try to colonize the whole world into believing what he believes.

Another important step to success is action. When you attend seminars, do you come back home to practice those things that you have been taught? Do you ever put to use those things that you know? You might as well know so much and yet your life remains the same simply because you put nothing into practice.

If you believe in something, isn't that enough calculated risk for you to act on? That is for instance, if you are a business man, lets say you produce goods, isn't your products good enough for you to bet on in the market?

If you know how correct your idea about a thing is, what stops you from betting on it? Your determination to win at all cost is what makes you a winner, a great man, a conqueror, an achiever and so many more.

Again the following are the steps to success
➢ Discovering your potential, instruments or abilities.
➢ Development.
➢ Determination to succeed

The three steps above are very important. It is what differentiates a success from a failure. Please observe them.

CHAPTER 9

There is No Reason to Cry in Pains. Just Look Into Yourself and Appreciate What You've Got and Happiness Would Come Your Way.

The number one thing everyone desire in life is happiness irrespective of who you are. You might be a rich man or a poor man, girl or boy young or old, all we seek is happiness. The reason why we do the things that we do all boils down to happiness.

If you are in school, that's because you want to obtain a certificate. The reason for the certificate is to use it to get a job. Why do you want to work? It's obvious you want to earn some money because you got some bills to pay or list of wants that you need to get for yourself. Whatever you will do with your money or whatever you will buy with your money is as a result of the pleasure you will derive for having that thing, it might be a car, you need it so you can easily move about, it still boils down to being comfortable and when you are comfortable, you are happy.

I have watched the interview of famous musicians and movie stars and there is this question they are always asked and they all seemed to be giving the same answer. The question is: "why do you do what you do?" And the answer they seem to always give is: "it is my passion for it" some says I've always wanted to be a movie star or a musician. So if a musician tells you that he is a musician because of the passion he has for music, he is simply telling you that music is what gives him happiness.

It is possible that these movie stars or the musician do what they do because of the huge money they stand to make but you will also agree with me that most of them like what they do because that's what give them the fulfillment they've been craving for.

When you see the musician and movie stars on T.V, don't they look like people who are fulfilled? Of course they act like they are the happiest people ever on planet earth. Almost every time you see them, they are cheered up. An entertainer is someone who derives joy in making other people happy. They are happy when they make others happy.

However, the musician and the movie stars or the entertainment industry is not the only industry where people derive joy. Another profession I would like to use as a case is the "teaching profession". Teachers and lecturers in highly industrialized nations may be well paid more than their counterparts in less developed nations of Africa but yet you find people who derive pleasure in teaching or lecturing even in the poor countries. They are fulfilled to see students knowing more than what they already know. Even their counterparts in the highly developed countries, teach because of the joy they derive from teaching.

The fact is when you see a person doing what he or she finds fulfillment, you will know. When you see a farmer that likes his job, you will know or a cleaner at restaurant. You will know because of how they go about their job. When you see a man who does not like what he or she does or where they work, you will also know. They treat their job with "I don't care attitude". They do not strife to get the best out of the job. Even when you are making so much money, once you cannot find passion in what you do, there is no need to continue. Majority of the world's population are facing this kind of problem. I know money is needed but can't you just find an avenue where you can be happy making the money?

There is no reason to cry in pains, why? There is a solution for every problem. Your case is no exception. All you have to do is to find out what truly makes you happy. Forget about the a whole lot of goodies, money or benefits you may be deriving from your current state of being, no amount of these things can buy you the happiness or fulfillment that you sincerely crave for.

It is not too late to go back your steps. As far as you still breathe, do it now. Do not prospone it, it's got to be now. Think about the days when you were younger, what did you dream to be? Or what is it that you've always wanted to be before you started deviating because of condition or circumstances. Instead of blaming your unfulfilled life on condition, why don't you start now, to make the right step? It is the only way you can ensure your happiness.

Begin now, to appreciate all that God has given you. There is nothing that you have that is of your own power so why don't you give praises to the giver–God? I am telling you this because I know how it feels like when you find yourself in a place where you don't want to be even if it may be paradise. There are a lot of rich kids who are tired and bored of their parent's mansion. Every minute, they are looking for how they can get out.

I know of some parents; they are so rich that they considered some professions low-class and as a result, their child must not learn any of such profession irrespective of their passion for it. That may be your case but instead you can find a way to be the best in whatever profession you find yourself and

CHAPTER 10

It's Easy to Break a Broom Stick but Impossible to break its Bunch. That Proves That Unity is Strength.

What is strength? And what is unity? These are the two most important areas we must find answers to as far as this chapter is concern. So first we will consider strength and then unity. Strength according to the oxford advance learner's dictionary has up to about ten (10) meaning but we are going to work with six.

1. **Being Physically Strong:** i.e. the quality of being physically strong
2. **The Ability:** That something has to resist force or hold heavy weights without breaking or being damaged.
3. **Being brave:** i.e. the quality of being brave, being determined in a difficult situation.
4. **Power/influence:** i.e. the power and influence that somebody or something has.
5. **Of opinion or feeling:** i.e. how strong or deeply felt opinion or a feeling is
6. **Advantage:** i.e. a quality or ability that a person or thing has that gives them an advantage.

From the six definitions above, we can see that they all talk about one thing: the ability to conquer or to dominate. So strength has to do with winning. It has to do with how many you had fought and how many you've been able to conquer. This is how strength is being measured.

How much or how far your influence can go in effecting a change in a matter that has to do with you or your environment directly or indirectly.

Now, let's go over to finding the meaning of unity after which we would discuss strength and unity together. By then it will be clearer.

According to the oxford advance learners dictionary, here we are given up to four (4) meaning but we will limit ourselves to only three (3) out of the four. They are as follows:
1. Unity is the state of being in agreement and working together; the state as being formed together to form one unit.
2. Unity is the state of looking or being complete in a natural and pleasing way.
3. Unity is a simple thing that may consist of a member of different part i.e. if a society exist in unity its members must have shared values.

If you have observed, you will notice one common thing being talked about here is "togetherness". The three (3) definitions all talks about being one in agreement.

So if strength has to do with the ability to conquer or to dominate and unity is about being one or together that means that ones you are in unity, you have strength. Once you are two or more together or in an agreement, you will be able to conquer and dominate. As far as I am concerned, this is the best kind of strength ever.

Imagine every human has its area of strength and uniqueness and then, more than two, it could be more than hundred, thousand or even communities, nations and countries coming together in agreement to join forces. Don't you think that they will be undefeatable? We are talking about thousands if not millions of skills coming together against one individual country. This kind of strength is the one that the broom has. The more the broom sticks, the more they become unbreakable.

Can you think of a major achievement you achieved alone without a help from someone else? I bet you that you will think all day and you would not be able to remember any. The truth is: there is no thing you've been able to do on your own without a help from another person directly or in directly, it could be an idea or advice that someone else helped you with. At the first place, the knowledge you have didn't just fall on you, you are a product of school or one learning institute or the other. You learnt from numerous teachers since you've been born.

Everything that you know today is as a result of the series of knowledge you gained from other people. As humans, we always learn from ourselves. That's why one should be careful about the kind of people you hang around with. They will go a long way to affect the kind of things that you learn.

This explains the reason or purpose of United Nations Organization. Many sovereign nations needed to come together in unity. Make out time on your own to read about UNO? Find out for yourself its objectives and the circumstance that led to her establishment. You will understand that everything boils down to being in unity so as to be stronger in order to maintain peace. If one member country disobeys, the others will come together against her and because they are many, they dominate and they also conquer.

Another thing that you will agree with me is that most times strength brings about peace. Since the UNO had been formed, peace now reigns to some extent. I think the level of peace between countries has increase tremendously. Unity has brought about strength and the strength in turn brought about peace. Now no one nation or country can prove to be stronger than the rest of the other countries.

Unity is strength, naturally you know this, if not then why is it that one person do not make a team, one person do not make couple, do not make a company, do not make a school, do not make a country, one person do not even make a family.

Let's take the football game for example, there is the coach, the keeper, the midfielder, striker and many more. Everyone perform best at his or her spot and at the end they win. They win because everyone did his or her part very well and that is the unity when a team is awarded the best team, it isn't necessarily because of their numbers or skills but as result of their level of cooperation. When the level of cooperation (unity) is very high, they can even beat down another team with multi talents. What is the use of a team being packed full with too many talents, if the too many talents cannot defeat a normal team full of cooperation?

Am sure that by now you must have understood what I mean by unity is strength. So don't just understand and sit there doing nothing about it but let it be your practice and you will surely reap its numerous benefits.

CHAPTER 11

Your Life is Like a Rent, One Day You're Going to evacuate it and Give an Account of How You Lived it. Do Not Ever Forget This While on Earth.

You know how rent is: it always involves two parties. One party is the owner of the property to be rented out and the other is the possessor of the property. Terms and condition always applies to rent.

If you have lived in a rented apartment before or still living in a rented apartment, you will probably understand me better what I have to explain here. When you decided to stay in the house or make use of the house, I am sure you met the land lord first or his agent; when you met him, he gave you the conditions to which you must adhere to before you can be given the space. Then you paid the amount and also signed the contract meaning you have agreed to all the terms and conditions that applied. What I am saying to you is that the life that you have was rented in that same manner but in this case you can't even pay money for it, the only way is to comply with its terms and conditions.

I assume that you know the life you have is not your own. At least this is the first thing you have to believe if at all we are to proceed. You did not create yourself. No! Someone else known as God created you and everything you have also comes from him. So now, the question is "have you ever asked or made efforts to know the terms and condition that applies to your life?

God created you and brought you into this world, he gave you breath, gave you special skills, talent within you and every day you sleep and wake up into a new day, have you ever ask yourself why did He create you or why is it that He still spares your life every day? Remember we are in a world that nothing goes for anything or do you believe that God just created you to be living and doing your own things? Of course no!

To some He gave one talent, to some others, He gave two talents and so on and so forth. Lets assume you have realize your own talent and it is dancing, are you dancing to fulfill the purpose why he gave you dancing as a talent?

The Purpose
Purpose in this context refers to terms and condition. The person who rents an apartment from a land lord was presented with options. The options were either for them to accept and be given the apartment or go away. This is why it is more accurate to refer to it as terms and condition but in this case that has to do with God, you don't have an option. Already you've been born so the only option remaining is for you to comply or else you would be burned.

The purpose every human is born into the world is to glorify God here on earth. What vary are the different instruments we've been blessed with to use in fulfilling this purpose. By now, you ought to have found out the kind of instrument you have. Make sure you are using it to glorify God no matter what it may be. God does not care. It is supposed to be used to glorify him.

Like I said earlier on, this rent from God, you have no control over its terms and conditions. You are left with one option, just an option which is to glorify God with whatever He has given to you. Another big difference between this kind of rent and the one between you and your landlord is that you know the date of expiration of the agreement but with God you do not know. It might be next hour or next day, you will be called upon to give an account. The question is: are you ready to receive the call of your master at anytime? If you are, that is good but if you are not, what are you still waiting for? Start making preparations.

How to Prepare

There are some important steps you need to take in order to be prepared. I will list them below and you should observe them thoroughly. The first three (3) steps have to do with you believing them. Just sincerely believe from your heart and accept them. The last two steps have to do with how you should behave after you must have accepted the truth. Below are the five (5) steps.
1. God exist, He created you.
2. He gave you everything that you have
3. There's a purpose why you are created
4. Ask God for guidance
5. Action (do his commands).

God Exist, He Created You

Believe sincerely from your heart that God exist. Even scientists at one time or the other have said that there is a supernatural being somewhere that is behind the creation of the universe. So all what scientists have been doing is trying to decode laws of nature and its properties in order to be able to connect them into very useful instruments that can better mankind.

For the fact that you know you didn't create yourself, neither did your mum or your ancestor did, should be enough for you to believe that there is a God somewhere who made all things and gave them all, laws to obey. For instance the law of reproduction, God made man and woman and commanded that whenever they come together, one thing or the other should take place in the woman's body and that should lead to pregnancy. We are the products of the law of reproduction. That's how I and you have come about so if you were to trace our origin, then you can trace it back to our maker which is God.

There's a Purpose for Your Creation
Look around you for anything that you have that is not fulfilling any purpose in your life. Truth is there is none. Anything you have ever tried to have has a purpose for which you wanted to have it for. That's the same way God created you; not just for creating sake but for a purpose. God felt the need of you in a particular place or aspect of life and he decided to send you down there.

One question you should ask yourself is that why are you born black or why are you born white? Why are you born in the place that you were born? And why are you the nationality of that country that you are? Why not another country? There is a reason for all this. The reason is to help improve human-kind in order to glorify his name.

He Gave You Everything That You Have
Everything that you have, he gave you. None you've been able to get on your own. Everything comes from him. For instance if you say you are a banker and the money you made comes from your banking job, question is: who made you a banker? if you should say you went to school and studied hard to become a banker, question is: who gave you the wisdom and the other resources? and then, if you should say that they came from your parents, question is: who gave your parent? If you continue to trace it like this, you will find out that God has been responsible for all your needs.

Ask God for Guidance

Now that you know your purpose on earth is to do wonders that will help human kind in order to glorify God? Believe me that same master that has sent you will also know the way you should go about it. So ask him for guidance and he will guide you right.

This time is a time to look into you. It is a time whereby some voice would began to speak to you; the voice of God and the voice of Satan. Listen carefully to be able to identify the voice of God. I believe the voice of God is gentler when you take it, you will feel a conviction that you are on the right track. Actually, at this stage, you need your pastor to counsel you

Action (Do His Command)

By now, you've listened or been listening, be determined to do the right things always. Always look for how you can use whatever you have to glorify God. When people see how much you are shinning, always be glad to inform them that it is by the handwork of God. By this, you are sending glories to his name and He will continue to bless you.

If you do all this, the lord will be pleased with you and whenever you depart from the world and are called upon to account, you will be guaranteed a place in heaven.

CHAPTER 12

It Takes Two to fall in Love or Else it becomes a Dangerous Affair.

Back in the days so long ago, there was nothing like money but the people still traded. They traded by means of trade by barter. Trade by barter is a type of trade involving two people. They do this by exchanging each other goods. For example, if Mr. A has a tuber of yam but he wants a gallon of groundnut oil, he will then have to look out for someone who has a gallon of groundnut oil and will be willing to exchange it with his tubers of yam. This was how our ancestors traded before the introduction of money and currencies.

But now, whatever you can get depends on how much that you have. So there is no need for exchanging goods for goods. One thing I'll let you know is that when it comes to love, we go back to the old way of trading which is trade by barter. This is even more serious because you will not just be exchanging any kind of good for another but the same kind of goods.

Love is so beautiful. In fact, it is the greatest gift one can get because money cannot buy it. But it becomes very dangerous when it is not a two way thing. It involves usually two parties and these two parities must show equal commitment because problems starts the moment one party is less concerned.

I have seen a very strong man, break down, I have also seen a very beautiful woman break down. I have seen boys and girls break down all because of wrong love partners.

I have seen very successful men and women loosing concentration all because they loved the wrong person who doesn't love them back. Many great men and women didn't do greatly in their love lives and that in a way, disturbed them.

Love has to do with the heart because it has to do with feelings of emotions and this is a very strong kind of feeling. It is a kind of a feeling that can change everything in one's life. Its organ of reasoning is not the brain but the hearts. It makes you want to always do anything for the person you feel it for.

I am sure that you will agree with me that the heart is one of the most important organs that we have. Anything that gets to the heart has gotten to us for real and so we should be careful what we allow to get to the heart. I'm not saying do not love. As a matter of fact we can't do without love. One way or the other, what keeps us moving is the love that we got from other people. The point here is that you should but the kind of love you fall into should be constructive love; not a destructive love?

A constructive love is a good love, it is the ideal love. It has a way of bringing out the best in us. Constructive means intended to be helpful or likely to produce good results. Some men have risen to the top because of the type of woman they married. Some women too have risen to the top because of love shown to them by their husbands. This is what love should be all about-helping each other to get to the top. Let it be that your partner is happy when he or she sees you happy. Any one of you pain becomes both of you pains and anyone of you joy because the both of you joy. By that you live as one, go though the same thing. Let both of you become an inseparable team. You labor together and also enjoy together. It is not necessary for both of you to always do the same thing but let it be that whatever both of you do, is for each other benefit.

When God created Adam-the first man, he also created Eve- the first woman. God made her with one of Adam's rib. This is the story of creation and it can be found in the bible in the whole of the book of Genesis. Please Endeavour to go and read it for more understanding. There in Genesis chapter 2:18, says "And the lord God said, it is not good that the man should be alone; I will make him an help mate for him". This implies that;

1.   To love is our nature
2.   Two people in love are help mates

The reason for Eve existence was to help Adam. Everywhere Adam exploits in the garden, she exploited it with him. Their goals were one because even though they were two creatures, but they were one.

There is just one essential thing in love; if it is not there at all, or involves both parties, the affair becomes dangerous. In love you must share. Adam and Eve shared. If you love someone and the person love you back and both of you share; the love becomes so sweet.

On the other hand, a love that involves one party or they don't share becomes destructive. To be destructive means intended to destroy. That's why a person who loves like this looses focus and you know what happens? Your career suffer set back or even total breakdown.

This has happened to many celebrities as a result of one party, stop sharing and this party stop sharing because he or she has stopped loving. Then when the other party notices this, he or she would start becoming emotionally distressed and before you know it, misunderstanding and series of problems sets in and they will start losing focus.

The question now is "how can we love constructively? The only time the aim and objectives of love can be met is when you love constructively. But remember you can only love constructively with the right partner. You need someone who can love you back as much as you do and be able to understand and care for you all the time. So this leads us to finding Mr. Right or miss right. Below are some useful steps you need to undertake.
1. Outline the qualities you want in the opposite sex
2. Do not rush into marriage
3. Seek the advice of a good counselor

Outline the Qualities You Want In the Opposite Sex
Everyman has a dream wife and every women have their dream husbands also. A dream husband or wife in the sense that the kind of person you would like to marry and be with all through the rest of your days on earth. There are some particular types of characters you want this person to exhibit. There is a particular form or shape you want this person to have. Sometimes you want the person to come from a particular type of background. These are what make up your dream woman or man. But the truth is: you cannot get all the qualities you want in just one person even though it is possible but why spend all your days searching for something you may never find.

So now, outline all the qualities you want in your dream partner. After that search for this person and when you find someone who has almost all the qualities, let's say more than half of the qualities you want, give this person a chance. Be friends with this person.

Do not rush into marriage
The mistake a lot of us makes is rushing into marriage without really knowing ourselves. The reason why we have dating is for

two people in love to use the period of dating in knowing each other and how to understand themselves. Dating is the period of time you should use to check if you guys would be compatible for life partners. If the answer is no, then you need to find a way to give yourselves a happy break up but if your answer is yes, then you can proceed further to engagement and then probably marry. Just make sure you are not rushing into marriage. let it be that truly during the period of dating or courtship, you guys discovered you are compatible to be life partners.

Seek the advice of a good counselor
The reason why there are counselors is for them to counsel us. We have counselors for various purposes but you should meet the one for love and relationship. The counselor would know what to tell or advice you. All you have to do is follow instructions. Any where you do not understand, ask questions so you can understand.

The three steps above will help you make the right life partner. This will further lead to reduce cases of divorce. When people who are compatible start dating and eventually marry themselves, the love between them becomes constructive and not destructive.

I know of many public office holders who have risen to the top because of the support they get from their partner. The same goes to so many preachers of the gospel. Any time you ask them, they are always willing to tell you that their back bone is their spouse.

I hope that you find the right person who will share the same aspirations with you; a person that you can understand and that will understand you also so that both of you would live happily together with all focus. "Finding the right life-partner gives you more chances of being great."

CHAPTER 13

Be Careful of the Kind and Type of Seed That You Sow Because It Will Also Determine the Kind and Type of Harvest You Shall Reap.

This is not hard to understand. It is simply telling you to lay your bed the way you want to lie on it. If you lay it rough, you will lie on it rough. But in case you don't like to sleep rough; you like to sleep cool, then you will have to lay your bed coolly before lying on it to sleep.

A farmer do not plant beans and expect to harvest rice unless he might have planted it. That is how life is in general. You only get what you work for and what you work for is what you deserve.

The phrase above talk about sowing seed; but not just that alone but also talking about the kind and type of seed. First, let's try to understand what it's being meant by seed before we go into kinds and types.

Usually a seed is that small hard thing produced by plants which a new plant can grow from. It is usually the beginning of life of something.

As humans, whether we like it or not, we are sowing seeds every day, sometimes knowingly and unknowingly and this seeds produced results for us. Have you ever notice it or wonder why you get wrong results or result that you did not just expect; this is because you must have sowed the wrong seed which produced the wrong result too.

Most of the seeds we sow unknowingly are the wrong seed and they produce wrong results. It is easier sowing bad seeds than good seeds. No wonder a saying goes "good things are hard to come by".

If you view the world, you will notice that very few are successful compared with the amount of failures? This is because a lot do not know what they are doing and where they are going. A lot are just following without even knowing what they are following. But the truth is every human being has its own destination and the earlier one discovers it, the better for him or she or you might go astray. The painful thing about going astray is that by the time you notice it, you might have gone too far to a point whereby to start tracing your way back takes a lot of time. Some have died while tracing their way back and that was the end. If you were already going astray before you discovered, to trace the right path, you must first of all come back to your starting point. This is time consuming but is better than not tracing your right path at all.

If there is a man who sends his kids to school, and there is another man who doesn't sends his kids to school, you will agree with me that both men are sowing different seeds and shall also reap different harvest. Action is action, whether it was done knowingly or not, it always have consequences.

Majority of students aims for the first class but very few gets it. It's usually like this because very few found the right seeds to sew. Every time we do something, just anything at all, we are sowing a seed. Our actions (i.e. seed) determines the kind of results (i.e. harvest). In life, everything is two; the bad and the good. What the quote meant by your kind of seed is whether your seed is good or bad.

A bad seed is the one that yield bad harvest. Bad harvest can be in any form. There is a saying that where there is no law, there is no sin and so therefore where there is no law, one can behave as he or she likes but fortunately in this world that we live in, there is a universal law which is "anything or activity that one embark on must be one way or the other beneficial to mankind". So any activity that does not aim at improving mankind is bad and so therefore its result or harvest shall be bad also. The law might not be written down anywhere but you and I know what the society or the world at large expect from us.

I see the world as a centre stage where everybody contributes their quota no matter how small it might be but that is what makes the performance complete and perfect. On the stage, the singer is needed and of course he can't do it alone, and so the drummer, has to come and help out, so as the pianist, the backup singers, the dancers and so on and so forth. Its either you belong to this or that but the most important thing is that you belong to one thing and that thing you belong to contributes positively to the performance. At the end of the day, you guys put up a great show. That is how the world is. Our little contributions go a long way.

Still on the music show as a case study, even the audience are contributing positively simply because they came. Some people in the world are just like those that never went for the music show. All they did was heard about how great the show went. When they finally crossed to the other side, nobody even knew. Only those that went for the show made impact.

"Selfishness is one of the world greatest problem and the greatest solution is selflessness."

Selfishness is the character of a man who thinks about himself only and does things that will benefit him only. Everything about a selfish man is himself alone. Everything is always all about him unless there's no going to be benefits. Picture a world where by every man fight for himself; their activities is only being guided by what they stand to benefit or gain, there will be no love, there will be no trust and there will be no peace. This is the kind of world the selfish people are trying to make. But the world would be better if there can be no more selfishness.

The aim of this chapter is to differentiate between bad seeds and good seeds and their harvests thereof. This advice is for everyone to embrace. Sow only the good seed so we can get only good harvest. Imagine a world whereby racism has no place, a world that believe in equality and due respect to every member, a world whereby every man is your brother and every lady is your sister without minding whether you are from the same background or share the same last name. Ask yourself this question and give yourself a honest answer, "wouldn't you like that kind of world?

That kind of world in our imagination can also be possible in the reality if we all share one particular policy which is the policy of selflessness. A direct and a complete opposite of selflessness is selfishness. We are the world. We are one big family. let's all embrace selflessness and the world would become a better place.

CHAPTER 14

If You Have Dream Without Problems, Then You Don't Really Have a Dream
                              - John Mason

Since the year 2000, I've always dreamed to be a star. I've always wanted to be a famous singer. I want to express myself through music and as well use my influence to make life more worth living for the people who are suffering to the extent that they can't afford common clean water. I've also dreamed to work with Michael Jackson-the king of Pop. Nine (9) years later he died when I've not even been ten thousand miles close to him. I felt really bad but still have to move on with the struggle of making my dreams come true.

It got to a time, it seemed as though nothing is working for me but I was made to understand that it is not the first straw that usually breaks the camel's back but the last one. So I believe I've not used the last straw and as long as I keep fighting, I'll get there.

I remembered when I published my first book - "love text massages and great quotes", I never knew publishing could be that tasking. I went through a lot. Suddenly all the little things became the biggest obstacles, that point I felt like its not my destiny to become a published author but somehow I pushed on and after some years I was able to publish for the first time at the age of twenty (20) years old.

For a dream to be a dream there must be problems. The road can't just be smooth. No! It must be rough. The rougher it is, the bigger the dream. Just like the greater the storm, the greater the reward.

Think about the dangers of climbing Mount Everest, the tallest maintain in the world. Think about the kind of hardship one is likely to go through just to get to the top of the mountain and tell me that the reward would not also be as great as how hard it was to get to its top. The measure of the reward is determined by how tasking it would be to get there.

Mount Everest was the highest mountain. It's more than 29,000 ft above sea level. Edward Hillary was the first man, to climb Mount Everest on May 29, 1952. One important thing to learn here is that Edward Hillary wasn't afraid of the height of Mount Everest. Even after he made an attempt in 1952 but failed, that only made him stronger in his skills and eventually the following year he made it to the top. As a result of his conquest, he was knighted for his effort with so many other benefits such as the recognition. Whether we like it or not, he has stamped his name in the book of world history.

Edward Hillary, I am sure wasn't the first to climb a mountain top nor the first to even make an attempt but he got more recognition for his effort because his dream was bigger, the storm was much more higher and so likewise it's reward.

A dream can't be normal: if it's normal, then it isn't a dream. A dream has to be something extra ordinary; I mean something abnormal so to speak at that current stage until you make it normal by achieving it. Let it be something that when people hear it, they will say "no it's not possible". The truth is everything that we enjoy today are as the result of someone else' dream. Before they existed, they were first being thought to be impossible but the great minds decided to make the impossible possible.

Look around you, every single thing was at some point impossible. Talk about the invention of the electric light by Thomas Edison, a German in 1881,

The evolution of motor car by Carl Benz a German in 1885,

The advent of the calculating machine by Charles Babage, an English man in 1855,

The invention of the television set by Hoan Logic Baild, a Scottish man in 1922,

The evolution of the airplane by Orville and Wright, an Americans in 1904,

The advent of the printing press by Johnann Gutenbery, a German in 1956,

The advent of the camera by William Fox Taibo, an English man in 1835,

The invention of so many other things that we make use of today were some other person's dream at a time

The question now is how can I conquer or what are the things I need to do in order to win? Below are two very important steps

1. Your dreams must be extraordinary
2. You must be brave.

Your Dream Must Be Extra-Ordinary

You will agree with me that as at 1881 or before then, anything like the electric bulb was an abnormal dream to have or the airplane before 1904 was an abomination to think of.

Do you also agree with me that as at before the year 2008, a African-American president was impossible? But Halleluiah! Thank God now, it's possible. It was somebody's dream many years ago: the person also was assassinated many years ago but the dream lived on and finally came true in the year 2008 when Barrack Obama became the first African-American president. What is it in life that you want to become?

How big is your dream? And what are people saying about your dream? If your dream is big, please enlarge it, make it bigger. If people say your dream is achievable, throw it away and construct another one. After then ask again and if they still say its achievable, throw it away also and construct another one. Continue to construct until they say it's impossible. Then you can say: you have a dream. A dream is not butter and bread neither is it cereals. Usually a dream is accompanied with thorns. The greater the dream, the greater its thorns and you will have to conquer its thorns before getting there. So make sure your dream is big enough.

You Must Be Brave
If you study the lion so closely, you will find out that it is very brave-be like it. Be used to problems, be used to obstacles, be used to tribulation and you will surely succeed. You will succeed because Jesus Christ went through all this and He still succeeded. So you can see that it's the price one has to pay for greatness. John Mason in his book: believe you can explained that:

> "The breakfast of champions is not cereal; it's obstacles and that the biggest successes are the people who solve the biggest problems".

They were able to solve their problems because they were brave and they solved this by willing to die for their cause. So are you ready to die for your dream? Your answer to this question will determine whether you will lose or make it. If your answer is no, you will lose and if you answer is yes, you shall surely make it. Even if you die for it, you shall surely still make it in death. Martin Luther king made his dream come true in death. He's still being remembered long after he's dead and he is still going to be remembered until Jesus Christ comes again. Emulate his bravery and you'll never regret it.

CHAPTER 15

We Make a Living By What We Get, But We Make A Life By What We Give.
- Norman MacEwan

These are two options for you. Among the two, one is greater and the greater says: we make a life by what we give. This is simply telling us to invest in others. The gain of the man that invests in others is greater than the one who invested in himself alone.

I am not saying that you shouldn't invest in yourself, but invest more into others for this is greater as well as its reward. Be selfless and not selfish. Ask yourself "what can I give to my community? What can I give to my state? What can I give to my country? What can I give to the world? And what can I give to improve or better human kind?

You will agree with me that there is no way you will improve human kind, without affecting lives positively. The more lives you affect positively, the more lives you make and the longer you will be remembered. There are some names you and I know that can never ever be wiped away from the surfaces of the earth until Christ comes again. These are the names that the bearers gave significantly while alive.

When it comes to making a life, sacrifice is the key, not the kind of sacrifice of Caine but the kind of sacrifice of Abel. I mean that type of sacrifices that represents the best of your bests. I bet you, when you give a sacrifice like this, you can never regret it. If you want to know better, ask Nelson Mandela.

Nelson loves his country so much that he was ever willing to give up everything for his country to be better. He was ready to pay the price so that his country could be transformed to the country he dreamed it to be. Nelson Mandela today is the greatest African patriot I've ever known.

CHAPTER 16

A Successful Man Is One Who Can Lay A Firm Foundation With The Bricks That Others Throw At Him
- John Mason

First of all, let's try to know what it means to be a success. The word "successful" means different things to different people but one thing I can assure you that in everybody's dictionary it means something positive and that agrees with our conscience.

Many has attempted to define the world "success" and thereby giving it many definitions. This is due to the fact that we are differently unique people with different perspective and perception.

However, one of my favorite definitions of the word "success" is that of the longman active study dictionary which defined it as "when you achieve what you have been trying to do" this definition is short and straight forward.

The other key word we need to examine very well here is the word **"bricks"** usually a brick is a hard block usually baked and used for building walls, house etc. Brick being used in this context is referring to obstacles, criticism, inconveniencies and so on. These kinds of bricks, you can't throw it to yourself. Others throw it to you in attempt to hunt you down. Some people throw bricks on you for good intentions but majority for had intention. This kind of bricks being throw to you are intended to damage you but where you become successful is your ability of being able to dodge them from hitting you, catching them and using them to lay a firm foundation but how?

Below are the following steps to take to be able to lay a firm foundation with bricks being throw at you.
1. Ask God for help.
2. Always see the brighter side of situations.
3. Be patient and steadfast.

Ask God for Help
The truth is most of those bricks are spiritual ones. The normal eyes don't see them. What you can only see is the havoc the bricks might have caused and so therefore you need a hand that is higher to help you out and that hand is that of God.

Right from the day you were born, everything you might have achieved is not by your might or power but by the grace of God who has created you and loved you even before you were born. So don't be afraid to always ask of help from him.

Another form of this bricks comes in a way of destructive criticism. There is what we call constructive criticism and destructive criticism. The difference is that while constructive is intended to sharpen your skills, destructive is intended to kill them.

There are a lot of people that would have been very great but the fear of criticism crumbled them. The great men and women you know today faced a lot of criticism but what made the difference was their ability to make a firm foundation with the criticism being thrown at them. I am not trying to say it's easy but that's why you need to ask for the strength to carry on. As a Christian, ask in the name of Christ and it shall be given unto you.

Have you ever been criticized before? The answer will be probably yes. At one stage of your life or the other, you must have done something that warranted a lot of criticisms. Even friends and families criticized you and during that period, you feel so abandoned and I'm sure you wished to turn back the hands of time so you can undo what you did but somehow after a while, what you did that brought you so much criticism later brought friends and families back to thank you. The great men and women that you know today have been through this kind of situation before many times.

You know, everybody call the name of Jesus; but do you know how much criticism and hatred he passed through? He was so much hated and criticized that they wanted him dead but that didn't make him change his mind. If Jesus, the only son of God had passed through it before, who says you can't pass through and succeed like He did? All you have to do is to ask for his wisdom, guidiance and follow His lead.

Always See the Better Side of Situation
Life generally has two sides-the "problem part and the solution part", the "labor part and the enjoyment part, the "sorrowful part and the happy part" and so on. The reason is that if you've ever been through the first part that seemed negative, you would appreciate the second part better which seemed more positive. Actually it's the side everyone wants to be.

I should have called the first side "bad" while the second part "good" but I leant that no side is bad. As a matter of fact, the most important part is the first part. I know that by now somebody will be asking why. I'll tell you why but first, answer this question analytically. "Why is there always a celebration after victory and a battle before victory?

You will agree with me that the battle gave birth to victory and victory gave birth to the celebration so the battle is the grandmother, victory is the mother and celebration is their child.

Problems will always be there and the solution finders will always be great also. Without problems, there would not be solutions.

All you have to do is to develop a good or the right attitude towards any situation you find yourself.

There is no genuine opportunity that does not come in a disguised form. Just as gifts comes with wrapper and you need to take your time to tear off the wrapper.

There are more problems in the world than there are living things and if the total amount of problems be divided by total amount of living things, i.e., each human being would still be having so much allocation of problems begging him for answers. What this means is that each and every one of us has an obligation to contribute our quota by solving at least one particular problem. The bigger the problem, the bigger the reward would always be also. You cannot be great without filling a vacuum and in the process people will discriminate against you. Other factors would try to stop you but know that it is only the tree with fruits that get being stoned and yet, it doesn't stop the tree from producing every season. When people throw bricks at you, don't complain and quit, instead lay a firm foundation with the bricks being thrown at you.

CHAPTER 17

It Only Takes a Small Courage to Start, But a Big Daily Dose of It to Keep Going, Because You'll Feel Like quitting A Thousand Times before You Get to the Top
                                                            - Bob Gass

By now it should no longer be a new word because it is a popular and well-known fact that "nothing good comes easy". Every made man you are opportune to meet and interact with, will tell you that to get to where he or she is took a lot of hard work. I know some of us will say that it is a lot easier now due to the advancement in technology and in scientific researches, but let no man deceive you. You still need to work hard to get anything good.

My first book was "love text messages and great quotes"; only I and God knows how many times that I wanted to quit writing the book. Even after I'd completed the manuscript, I went through a lot of obstacles just to get it published, there I gave up even more times that I gave up while still trying to complete the manuscript.

The moment you want to use something for something good, it becomes hard to get. I can still remember how many times that I hard to write my exams with just one biro. No extra biro by my side for incase the one I'm using stops. This happens not because I didn't make provision for extra biro but what happens is that during normal classes I always have up to about three basically. You will have something in excess but when you truly need it, the case may become different.

A better example of this is love. A love may be knocking on your door when you don't need it. Sometimes love knocks at your door when you are already busy with another love. Sometimes it could take you so long to realize it but the moment you realize it, it's gone and you'll now be the one searching for it.

Please, if you meet Michael Jordan, help me ask him how many times he has lost. Probably it will be more than how many times he had got three points on the ring and that means that he must have been surviving with more courage each day.

Many had tried but failed; not because they couldn't do it but because they did not produce more encouragement for themselves in order to get ahead. What made them tried at the first place was the encouragement but later failed because they didn't get more of the encouragement.

The truth remains that it's easier to be at the bottom than to be at the top. A typical example is mountain climbing. The higher you go, the tougher it becomes. You just have to develop your skills and try to manipulate the circumstance to favor you so you can conquer.

According to Bob Gass, in his book, "forgetting your past pg 28", he said that the courage you need to keep on moving comes from three things which are:
1. The book you read
2. The relationship you form, and
3. The time you spend with God.

The Books You Read
A lot of knowledge is deposited into books. Anything at all that somebody wants to become has a book that gives its guidelines. This is the reason why you need to know your purpose for living so that you can focus well on the things that will help

bring out the best in you. Great men reads and leaders read because a good reader makes a good leader.

I advice that you read very wide so that you can be versatile. But spend more time on your domain. I, personally, books have helped me a lot. Everything can't come from your tutors. So you dig when you read. Right from time I know that to be a good writer, you have to be a good reader.

The reading aspect is just step one. It is not complete if you do not practice what you read. Sometimes people read these motivational books and find out about a lot of secrete to success and the various steps needed to take but failed to practicalize these steps. As a result, they remain where they were and later get even more depressed. That's when you start to hear them say stuffs like "motivational books don't work" or "do not waste your time reading them". Most people you see on top of their game are good readers who do not only read but also practicalize what they read.

The Relationship You Form
Your friends either make you or break you. Who you associate with matters a lot. Evil mind corrupts good mind. Everything that you know today or that you do now was learnt from someone you once had a contact with. There is nothing you must have learned on your own. This is how we human beings influence ourselves uncautiously.

There is an adage that goes this way: "show me your friend and I'll tell you who you are". Sometimes you associate with people even when you know very well that the person's direction is different from yours. We do this all in the name of hoping to change the person but the person ends up changing us.

Those that you see last before you sleep every night and those that you mingle with first in the morning when you wake up always have a strong influence on you.

CHAPTER 18

The Rich Man Has A Language... So Also Is the Poor Man

Language is a tool for communication. It is normal for various dictionaries to give various meaning because they varies but one thing I am very sure is that it boils down to communication.

Communication is very broad and so we are not concerned with it as a whole but as an individual who communicates with his neighbor, peers immediate family etc.

When we say "the rich man" it may not necessarily be the man with so much money. He that has ideas capable of being transformed into a milestone is who I call a rich man. One may be asking now "what about the poor man"

I call him who lacks initiative, the poor man. How can one ever move without a foresight? it's wrong.

Rich man or poor man, they both have their languages. I don't mean their tribal languages, what I mean is the language as a result of their level of thinking. There is a place in the bible that says: "whatever a man thinketh in his heart so he is". This is nothing but the gospel truth. Out of the abundance of the heart, mind speaketh through the mouth. There is nothing one does without first doing it in his mind or having a conceptual model of it.

The Rich Man Language

Truly the rich man language is a highly prestigious language. It is not meant for all. In fact it is meant for a selected few. Have you ever wondered why the workers in the church, If all put together cannot still be up to half the numbers of the congregation?, the numbers of artist billed to perform in a concert no matter how many, cannot be up to half the number of the crowds that will show down, have you ever wondered why there are fewer billionaires than millionaires, fewer millionaires than thousand naires? In an organization, the higher the level, the fewer the people. No matter how many politicians are in a country, they can never be up to half the population of the country.

Another unique feature of the rich man's language is that it intimidates. For instance, silver intimidates bronze, Gold intimidates silver, and diamond intimidates Gold.

The poor man is intimidated each time the rich man speaks. And so the poor man grumbles. Sometimes he complains that the rich man is proud whereas the rich man is just saying it the way it is. For instance, the rich man, when telling a story, he makes mention of flashy things that expresses his luxurious life style even when he doesn't want to sound so intimidating. He might tell you a story of a mishap when he was in the jet flying, meanwhile the poor man's story of a mishap could be in the train when he was going to work. You see, that's the difference.

Another thing about the rich man is that he speaks more positivity than the poor man.

Now ask yourself this question: "which of the language is more prestigious to speak? Of course it is the rich man's language but why then do you say he is proud?

Who is the rich man?
The rich man has a lot of money, a lot of valuables. Yes! But that is not who he is.

The rich man is one with a foresight and initiatives. According to the long man active study dictionary, foresight is the ability to imagine what might happen in the future, and considers this in your plan.

The future is for those who planned for it. I know luck has a role to play but you first, have to be on your "get set" waiting for luck to tell you "Go!" and then you go and conquer. Later, people would start saying that you are a lucky man or woman because you've made it but the truth is that you couldn't have made it if you were not prepared for it. All these while, you've been like an athlete on a track, you have passed through the stage of getting on your mark and set, you are ready to go but have been patiently waiting to hear the sound of the gun shot.

The poor man's language is so much of negativity such as "I can't do it, I'm afraid, and so on and so forth. The language portrays a picture of a man or a woman with little or no vision.

Ask the poor man how is tomorrow going to be like? He will tell you, "I don't know" and sometimes when they speak like this, they believe they are being humble but that's wrong.

Now, ask the rich man that same question. You would get such answers as "I'm going to be traveling, I'm going to be at home with my family, etc there is a lot of I'm going...to in the rich man's language which signify the presence of plans for the future.

No man makes progress without plan and not just a plan but a very good plan. Only then, can we find ourselves speaking the rich man's language and that's the one we should all work hard to speak.

CHAPTER 19

When You Try To Spend Less, You End Up Spending More

Life situations have taught me that whenever we try to spend less, we end up spending more. When I was growing up, my grandmother always told me "never to pass short cuts".

We spent more time looking for a short cut when we should have actually taken the time to go though the normal way that everyone know?.

Reasons Why You Should Forget About Short Cuts

It is time consuming
A lot of time would be spent on trials and errors whereas you haven't even started. The man who is passing through the generally-known route had been moving all this while that you were wasting time doing trials by errors in order to discover a short cut.

You don't know where it leads
Let us assume you have found the short cut, but you don't know where it leads and if you would pass through it, you don't even know where you are going to burst out from.

You may miss your survival training
People who pass through short cuts also end up passing out so soon. There's a saying that goes like this "easy come, easy go" and nothing good comes easy. A good meal actually takes longer to heat up or to prepare. You can ask Gordon Ramsay if you like.

When you take the normal way, you would have the opportunity of going through a lot of training. Although, training might be very stressful and challenging, it prepares you for the task ahead. I know of many people who got to the top so fast but lacked the necessary requirements needed to stay on top and in no time, made their way back to the bottom.

In other words, the man who made arrangement for little, most time ends up incurring more. When you go to the super market to buy groceries, you find out, the more that you have bought, the higher the discount that you are being given and so the man who had bought a lot would probably go home with enough groceries at a lower rate. But the man who came and bought very few would receive very low discount rate and by the time he gets home, he finds out that what he had bought would not be enough for the family and so he makes his way back to the store and buy little again with little discount rate being given. Between these two people, the one that budgeted to spend more ended up paying lesser and the one who tried to spend less ended up paying higher price, his time and the stress of going back to the store anytime soon.

Smartness Is Not Short Cut
There are some people who believe or sees short cut as being smart. Smart is the act of being intelligent and sensible. With all the risks involved in short cut taking, no one can still say short cut taking is being smart.

When someone is intelligent and sensible, shortcut is not an option to him.

CHAPTER 20

Presence of love in our hearts makes us angels but lack of it turns us into monsters

Human beings by nature are monsters. They are so cruel and evil. Humans find it easier to steal and destroy than to build. We were born into an evil world by evil people with the sinful nature. With this, no good should be expected from us. But then God decided to provide us with an option of grace. He sent down his only begotten son to come and die for our sins so that we may be saved from the evil bondage that we are in and so therefore, anyone who gives back evil is on his own.

You see, everything God has done for us is always a demonstration of love. He teaches us to love because that is the only way we can be nice to others and ourselves. Love is said to be the greatest commandment of God and I believe.

When you do not love, you hate. Some people would say "I don't have hate but I just dislike" they are the same "dislike" is a fraction of hate just as "like" is a fraction of love.

Little children without being taught how to destroy already know how. But for them to know how to build, somebody would have to teach them first. But why?

The same people that we once loved and did everything for, when the love goes away, we are the same people who want to also destroy them. If a monster should fall in love, to the particular person he loves, he becomes an angel because it is only love that can take away the beast nature of man. This means that if we can love more people, the world would become a better place.

Most leaders are monsters because they don't have love for the people they are supposed to lead. A leader must love his people. Absence of love in his heart for his people means he can't make a good leader. There is space for competency but it is better to elect a leader who is not competent enough but loves the people than the one who is very competent but would not still be able to defend his people's interest. The not-too competent leader would serve his people better because of the love in his heart for them.

CHAPTER 21

Revenge makes you put more burdens on yourself than the actual one being put on you by another person

Most of the time we are hurt by the people we least expect would hurt us. People that we have trusted and love so much most time hurt us the most. There are some hurts that are so deep and they could take a life time to heal.

Human beings have always avoided being hurt and so they try to play safe but just when we least expect it, it's there again smelling around us and making us hate even the air that we breath.

The heart is the most precious organ of man. Whatever a man thinketh in his heart, so he is and so whatever gets to a man's heart becomes a serious issue.

The world we are today is so full of deceits, so filled with masked people, they live fake lives and if you are not wise enough, you will be deceived. But you cannot be wise over night, you need to experience some hurts by yourself, that way, you learn. You learn by getting over a heart break.

There was a man that once lived on earth. He never committed a crime or sin but one day, he was betrayed by one of his disciple. Eventually, he was laid on the cross after being subjected to so much humiliation and mockery. This man before he gave up the ghost on the cross, he prayed to God

Almighty, his father to forgive all those who had wronged him. His name is Jesus.

Forgiveness is like a scratch on your skin; you can easily endure the pain and after a while, it will heal by itself. But when you decide to revenge, you can't get your mind of the pain and the pain gradually starts to go deeper. From your skin to your flesh, your flesh to your bones and blood and at this point, it gets to your heart and you can no longer control it. Forgiveness becomes impossible but remember that when you point a finger at a person, the rest points back at you.

When you go back to revenge, it is like leaving a permanent scar and scars will always remind you of what happed before. The more you remember, the more you get hurt and this is for a lifetime till you forgive.

The devil has a way of packaging the ugliest things to look so beautiful and by the time you have made your purchase, you will find out that what is displayed on the body is actually different from what is inside but when you take it back for refund, the devil will deny you and even mock you. How long would you continue to allow the devil to mock you?

Steps to Avoiding Revenge

Get Your Mind of the Hurt
We are being wronged everyday but let us try to always get our minds of the wrongs being done to us. I understand that hurts can come in different degrees but they can all be forgotten.

Occupy your mind with the things that interest you the most. Those activities that makes you feel very light and happy, engage more in them.

Talk to someone
Talk to someone or people that you know will understand or at least make them understand your situation. They say "a problem shared is a problem have solved". And it's true.

When you talk to someone, there is a lightness that you feel. The wound you have would begin to now heal. When that happens, the pain or the hurt doesn't get to your heart.

Cry all the tears if you have to

This is another method that is very effective especially among women. Go to a very quiet place, shut the door, reminisce and start to cry. Allow the tears to flow out and do not ever try to fight to hold them back. Cry all your emotions out and you'll be stronger again. When you cry, have it at the back of your mind that it isn't your fault and that things were just met to happen that way because no one decides his or her destiny.

Hang Out

When you are done with crying, you need to hang out; not alone but with some friends and family members. Outdoor activities have a way of clearing ones head. Get some good fun.

CHAPTER 22

Become an Authority on Something
- John Mason

In life, there are so many aspects. They are all working together to achieve one aim. Life can also be regarded as a faculty with so many parts; all working towards the single direction of the whole faculty.

Let's take for instance, the faculty of management science in the university. The faculty has various departments such as the business management, accounting, finance and banking, marketing etc. Then, let's assume the goal of the faculty is to graduate the highest number of 1st class degree holders in the university next convocation. All the various departments would start to work towards achieving that goal of the faculty. The students in management would be learning something different from the other students in other department. This is because everyone needs to specialize in specific areas and become an authority in that area.

What I am trying to say is that we waste so much time and talent enjoying what others does and at the end, becomes an authority no where.

God has created each and every one of us to become an authority in at least one area of life. To some, he has giving one talent, two talents, three talents and more but life is not about what you have but by what you do with it.

If the man with just one talent utilizes his own very well, he is better of than the one with five talents who did nothing with them.

People look at other people and see only the strengths in them and they start to get envious. One thing you should know is that those that you envy also have weaknesses just as you do.

What you should do is to identify your talents and see how you can work on them, identify your weaknesses and see how you can cover them up with your strengths. That way, you shall thrive and not stay behind in the race of life.

Every strength that we have is designed towards solving a problem in a particular aspect of life. If you work and concentrate on your strength, you shall become an authority in that aspect.

To become an authority in a particular thing is not and can never be a day's job thing. You must realize that you need to work on it for several days, weeks, months and at times, years. Two major things you need to have are concentration and consistency.

CHAPTER 23

In life, there's no such thing as calculated risk because risk is risk; nothing less.

There's a man at the taxi park, he is a taxi driver and he is 60 years old. I'm not trying to discriminate against taxi cab drivers or the profession. Whatever you do, be the best; but I'm just trying to let you understand how people who had dreamt big ended up settling for less; all because they thought they were smart by trying to take only calculated risk.

Truth is, if the 60 year old man planed to take the ultimate risk, at 60 year old, he should have owned his own taxi cabs company and not driving just one all day.

The same thing goes to the manager in the grocery store. He has been a manager for so long now, don't you think it's time he goes and establish his own store?

Truth is: he is afraid of taking the ultimate risk of establishing his own grocery store and so he settle for less.

Low lifers have one mentality and it is "nothing at all is worse than none", it is every time they settle for little things and they say it is better than none; sometime hope for either nothing or the best and I bet you, you will surely get the best.

No man knows tomorrow
We are in a world where no one knows tomorrow. Companies spend so much on forecasting and yet they never get it accurately. When you say you are taking a calculated risk, it

means you must have forecasted how the future environment would be like and as a result, you have made your plans according to the forecast. What will happen if the events turn out to happen in the opposite direction? Would you quit? As at this point, you are probably more on the side of quitting because you had gotten more than you bargained for all in the name of calculated risk.

Make flexible plans
When you truly want to succeed in life, there should be nothing like calculated risk on your agenda. All you need to do to be successful is to be flexible like the cat. The cat easily reacts to changes in the environment.

You need plan A, B, C, D etc as many as you can make. May be when implementing plan A, something changed in the environment, you immediately switch to B.

Let your plans be adaptable, in order to suit little unforeseen changes.

Have a contingency plan also. If in the course of implementing a particular plan, an urgent need arises, you already know what to do and you should start doing it immediately. It is not time to start thinking of what to do; that's what makes it a contingency plan.

CHAPTER 24

When chasing your dreams, go for the standard your heart desires and do not ever try to compromise.

People have always settled for less for reason best known to them. When a man dream to become something great and later on settle for something less, it is as a result of so many factors acting against his will-power.

Will Power
This can be defined as the determination and the ability you have to focus or concentrate on something that you hope to achieve.

You need to boost your will-power even more than 100% if you can. It is a very vital characteristic if you must achieve your desired dreams.

Your will-power will help you to focus on your dream. It ignites the fire in you and makes every part of your body and soul to be aware of your dream. When your body and soul are awake, you become like a soldier; you are ready to go to war at any time you need to.

Your will-power would give you an extra-energy that even at times when you are supposed to be sleeping, you are working, when people doubts you, you are stronger and more determined because something in you want to prove them wrong –that's the extra energy at work.

The moment your will-power starts to drop, a lot of things start to go wrong. The body is notified that you are no longer as determined and focus as before and so therefore reduces the extra-energy being given to you. That's when you will find out that you have started sleeping at the normal time everyone sleeps, when people doubt you, you believe them and that thing inside of you doesn't seem to want to prove them wrong any more.

Before you know it, you will start to come down, you will start to make your dream smaller and finally settle for something less.

At times, to compromise is good; especially when two people who had been at war but are now ready to make peace. They would have to compromise individual interest a bit so that peace can reign. This situation is more like a case wherby someone brings out a hand for hand shake, the other party need to bring out his or her hand for the shake as well.

But in your career or individual aspirations, do not ever try to compromise. Always go for the best that you know.

Consistency

Consistency and will-power works together. In a situation whereby your will-power is high and you are very consistent in what you do, you can achieve anything.

That special person in your life, did him or her loved you all at once? of course no. Somebody confessed his or her love for the other person and the person was consistent in order to really prove it. Eventually, the other person had no choice than to give in. That's the same method you apply when trying to achieve anything.

Think about how you loved that man or woman; remember how consistent you were and so many other things you had to sacrifice. *In the bible, it is written that* the man who is diligent in his work shall sit amongst kings.

CHAPTER 25

In whatever chosen field of career that you find yourself, be a professional so you can grow.

In this chapter, in order to fully make us understand, I am going to use the office environment as a case study.

A lot of us that works in the office complain of no promotion or if there is, the promotion is not as fast as we want or feel it should be.

And we result to all manner of method. All in a bid to solving this problem of no or little promotion.

The question I want to ask is this: "have you searched within yourself whether you truly deserve promotion?" have you check your own level of productivity?

You, the employee, the firm sees you as the instrument she can use to achieve her aim, goals and objectives. In the other hand the employee sees the firm as a means through which he can settle his bills and live a fulfilled life. Now, this is the common interest both the firm and the employee have.

Based on this, the case is simple. If the employee is not productive enough, the firm would not regard him that much as well.

Below are guidelines to becoming a professional in your chosen filed of career.

Competence
You need to be competent enough for the job. This will increase

your confidence. It has to be a job that you are not struggling with but a job in your area of authority.

Many people have found themselves in places they never wanted to be before because maybe, it's the family business and so they must feel the void. This set of people usually live a life that is far from a fulfilled one.

Uphold the ethics of the profession

As we both know, all professions have their ethics. As a professional, you must uphold the ethics of your profession always. Ethics is like a moral duty you owe to the profession you are in.

A lot of us do not keep to the ethics of our profession and you think people or your boss is not watching? Of course someone is always watching. The question now is: how do you expect to be promoted when you do not even keep to the ethics of the profession. Even though, the company may be yours but I believe you belong to a particular union that has the right to sanction you. So one way or the other, you are getting no promotion when you don't keep to the ethics.

Minimize religious sentiments

Some people do not do what they ought to do. They spend the whole time praying when they are actually supposed to be proving their professionalism. You cannot grow or be promoted when all you do is your religious activities at the

CHAPTER 26

There Is More Vision Extinguisher Than Vision Molders.

Vision extinguishers are vision killers. If you let them take over, it means automatically your vision is dead. These set of people are unfulfilled. There are people who couldn't just make it or achieve it up to that point that you are aiming at and so they tends to discourage all those who dare try to dream or attempt it.

Some other people, their problem is just wickedness. Only them wants to shine and so only them deserves to achieve some things. That is what some people want; they go as far as helping only their kids.

There are very few of the world's population who enjoys helping others in getting to their highest aim. Usually what majority do is to help you to a point and leave you there and when they see that you are beginning to grow more than they predicted or expected, many of them become the unknown enemy. You need to be extremely careful about how you communicate your visions, dreams and goals to people.

Some People Must Never Know
The story of Joseph, the dreamer, son of Jacob in the Holy Bible is a very good example. According to Genesis chapter 37:1-36 Joseph, who was the 11th child of their father-Jacob, was the favorite of his father's children.

This young man had a dream that one day, he was in the field with his brothers, tying up bundles of wheat, suddenly his bundle stood up and the rest of his brothers bundles gathered around and bowed down to his own.

Another day again, he dreamt another dream and decided to tell it to his father, mother and brothers. Joseph said that he dreamt and the sun, the moon and eleven stars bowed down to him.

Reactions to Joseph Dreams
Of course after telling them his dreams, nobody called him for celebration and jubilation of what is yet to come.

His brothers hated him more after telling them his first dream. Again, he had another dream and gathered his parents and brothers to tell them. This time around even his father got angry but although he observed it and that's because it is the joy of every father for their children to achieve more than them. Joseph's brothers did not only hate him more but also planned how they can eliminate him entirely from the family picture.

Fortunate Joseph
Joseph made a mistake that could have led to the end of his life and dream. It was not just necessary to gather his entire family to tell them his dream. He would have called one or two persons to tell his dream to and somehow God would have still made it come through.

Joseph was fortunate to have enough of God's grace upon him and God made a way even when there was no way for him. God is God and his prophesies shall always come to pass. But what about others who may not have enough grace as Joseph?

Prevention Is Better Than Cure
Do everything you can, to prevent all misfortune. Do not leave

it to chance but when it has already happened, you can now seek for a solution.

Everyone have dream and so be careful how you go about disturbing others with yours. Sometimes it makes you look selfish and also for the purpose of avoiding unnecessary clash of interests. Save your energy for the accomplishment of your dreams by avoiding wasting energy and time in trying to tell everyone.

CHAPTER 27

God has given to us a minimum of one talent but the capacity to manage it properly does not always rest with us and that's why you need to look for your manager today.

A talent is a gift from God that enables you to perform some certain skills effortlessly or better than others.
When you have a particular talent, you will find out that, you perform that skill without really trying so hard. It is something you do with a natural enthusiasm. This means that you do not get tired doing it.

I have research and find out that all human beings are unique in different ways depending on the particular thing God has placed in you.

If you are still there wondering if you have a special talent, then you are wasting your time because you have a minimum of one special talent. All you have to do is to ask God to open your eyes to see the beautiful thing he has placed in you. Don't ever abandon those things you once did with a burning fire from the inside of you, those things that you do effortlessly and that gives you natural peace and joy while doing them.

Steps to Discovering Your Talent

Make a visit to an authority
An authority is one who has expertise knowledge about a particular thing or field.
    Look for an authority in the area of talent identification and pay a visit to this person. He or she shall open your eyes to see your internal strengths and capabilities. Usually they will ask you very private question about your life but you need to trust and give the correct answers so they can be able to serve you better.

Learn To Listen To Your Inner Mind
Your inner mind is your conscience. Every human being has this and it speaks to us on a daily basis.
    Try more to stay in less noisy environment or better still, find time to be in a room alone, that's when the voice of your inner mind becomes louder for you to hear. If you can learn to identify and obey this inner mind voice, it will never lead you astray so try...

Remember Your Childhood Activities
I can still remember back in the days when we were in nursery, and then to primary, after graduation from primary, we moved to junior high school, there used to be some subjects that connects to my mind, body and soul that I usually pass effortlessly. There used to be some sport activities that I preferred doing than others, through this knowledge I was able to draft a proper career path. By the time I got to senior secondary school, I already know the subjects I am not supposed to play with. Many of my friends went into science, others joined because everybody seemed to be going there. But I went into commercial because it is where I love to be.

Managing Your Talent

After you must have discovered your talent, you need management. A manager is one who manages other people including their potentials and resources for the purpose of getting the best possible outcome. He is capable of bringing out the best out of your talent. He helps you to refine and develops it, thereby making it more appealing for marketing.

The devil pretends to be a manager or most times, a giver of talent but the truth is: God is the only giver of talent and the devil can only pretend to be its manager. The mistake people make is signing up to the devil to manage their talents forgetting that he, who has given them, also has the ability to manage it for them even more better.

The Capability to Manage Talent

The capability to manage what we have does not usually rest with us. We need others to succeed because no man is an Island.

Music and movie stars had crashed simply because they fired their manager or do not have good managers.

When you have a talent, you are like a brand. You and I know that coca-cola cannot manage itself.

Attributes of a Good Managers

Sincerity: A good manager needs to be very sincere with who he or she manages. Lies and insecurity has a way of tearing down good relationships and trust others have in us.

Interest at heart: A good manager would see your success as his and would do everything to make you succeed. He or she must have your interest at heart but believe in you.

Mother and child relationship: You may be the one paying your manager but in a way, he is like your father or mother. He forgives you every time you offend him knowing and unknowing and even when you do not apologies sometimes. If your manager holds some grudges against you, he will not be able to have your interest at heart.

CHAPTER 28

> Heaven helps those who help themselves.
> -Unknown

"Heaven help those who helps themselves". This is deeper than a lot of us think it is. This is actually telling you to do your own home work. The proverb is telling you as well to do your own personal work properly. If at all you will get help, you need to have started doing your own part.

In essence, you cannot be helped from nothing. It is your duty to lay the foundation and then you may be helped with the build-up.

Know What You Want
The first step is to know what you want. When a child knows what he or she want, he or she is able to cry very well for it and even when you bring another option, he will tell you no.

Knowing what you want will enable you to begin to plan on how to map out strategies that will enable you to achieve your aim.

Start a Plan
The next step after you've known what you want is planning with your resources in consideration. And then you outline your strengths and weakness and try to develop a formula that will help in using your strength to cover up for your weakness.

Give your plan a time frame. Let it have a particular or definite time of accomplishment.

Action
Action here refers to the performance of the strategy you must have mapped out. The carrying out of the plan must be done or else it amounts to no plan at all.

You must be able to stick to the plan, make some future changes if necessary and at the end of the day be able to evaluate your level of progress.

Existing Natural Laws
There are some existing natural laws that operate in the universe. There is a reward for every law followed. You must first of all observe these laws by keeping to them. To get a desired result, you must know which of the law to keep to.

As an achiever, when you do your part very well, nature naturally gives you what you deserve.

For instance, it is definite that a student who had prepared for his examination by setting out a good amount of time to read and understand before his examination day will surely make a very good grade.

As you can see, he had to do one thing for another thing to happen. He helped himself first by preparing and then heaven helped him further by making sure his effort is not in vain.

A young lady who was pregnant and decided to go and be checking on her doctor regularly to tell her the condition of her baby inside, finally put to bed safely. What do you think she has done? She has helped herself for heaven to help her.

You are responsible for every single thing that happens to you both bad and good. As a human being, you are one whole system. Tough situations can only hit you but cannot break you as long as you are keeping to the rules.

I am also aware that there are some situation you may find yourself, everything looks totally out of control, you still need to attempt finding a solution, when the spiritual bodies sees your efforts, they would become so glad to assist.

CHAPTER 29

The little things one does are what make the difference as long as you are consistent.

In a day, we have 24 hours and that time seemed short, truly it is short. No wonder people say time is short. From the 24 hours a day, you have a minimum sleep of about 5 hours; the remaining 19 hours is still not all yours because domestic issue would surely still take your time. Unnecessary delays are also there, some external variables that you have no control of are also there.

After subtracting the 5 hours sleep, we are left with 19 hours; from there we subtract time to bath, morning and night, the time spent ordering for a meal at the restaurant or cooking it ourselves, the queues at the bus stop, the traffic light delay, the time spent on trying to get from the bus stop to your office or place of destination. By the time, we subtract all this time consumed at various point or the order, from the remaining 19 hours, I doubt if we barely have up to 10 hours left.

Let's assume 10 hours is left from the 19 hours. Psychological issues may come to play but your ability in handling them shall save you.

This is where you need discipline or else you won't know when the whole of your remaining ten hours will be spent on socialization, keeping to unnecessary or unproductive dates.

You should be able to live the lifestyle that is modest so you can have enough time to focus.

The point here is **consistency**
Consistency is the quality of always behaving in a particular way or continuously doing one thing.

How consistent are you in those things you do in order to push forward in achieving your dreams?

By the time you answer this question, you would know the next step to take. If your dream is truly important to you to achieve, then you must give it a consistent focus.

If you are a professional dancer for instance, out of 24 hours, you only have 1 hour for your dance rehearsals and practice. That is considered very little a time one should give to his or her profession or career but let's now look at it from the angle of being consistent.

1 hour a day would give 7 hours a week. In a year, that would be 365 hours or 366 hours in a leap year.

Let's assume, you learn a new step or dance style per every rehearsal; that would be 365 new dance styles in a year.

Meanwhile, the man who rehearses for about 3-4 hours in a stretch but who is not consistent may be rehearsing 5 hours per week, sometimes it could be 3 hrs per/week and then in a year, he must have spent total of less than 300 hours on his dance rehearsals.

If he learns a new dance style every hour that he rehearse, that could be not more than 300 dance styles for him in an entire year.

From the above illustration, between the consistent and the non-consistent man, you know who is better. No one can be best without consistency. It could be the extra 15 minutes spent on training that will just make the difference.

All the world-best that I have known ranging from various professions such as in football soccer game, music, basket ball, athletics etc gave extra time to themselves.

In Relationship

The rule of consistency also applies to the relationship we have with other people.

CHAPTER 30

There is no problem that builds in a day. The day you noticed it is the day that it got matured meaning that it has been developing for a while.

Using tree as an example, the moment the branch is detached from the vine, the branch dies. But in some trees, the leaves on the branch could still look very fresh for about 7 days before they will start changing color.

The fact is that the detached branch died long time ago but it was taking just a matter of time to show itself so it can be noticed.

So many problems are still in disguise and the moment they are unraveled, we begin to think that it was that day it started.

I have witnessed how some relationships crashed, environments destroyed etc. erosion for instance does not start in a day. It could take up to two decades of negligence before it finally starts to become an environmental problem.

How to Avoid Problems

Be quick to identify
If one can identify a problem on time when it is still developing and yet to be matured, measures can easily be put in place to avoid it.

The major task in trying to identify problems on time is being very observant you should be able to analyze present situations and predict the problems they tend to create. Sometimes when we see a problem, we ignore simply because it has not gotten bigger.

Be proactive in response
After observing and finding out the problem that may occur, the question is what do you do? At this stage you should begin to think fast on the next step of action that could block the problem. When you know what to do and act on time; that is being proactive. For instance, when one travel with a spare tyre; that is being proactive.

Other Ways of Avoiding Problems
There are so many ways of avoiding problems depending on its nature. There are problems that are social, technological, and economical in nature and so on. These entire problems have different ways of being prevented from happening. Generally, there are ways of reducing one's problems and the two solutions explained above are the keys into solving any problem that may want to occur at all. No matter its nature, be it political, economical etc.

Adopt the lifestyle that suits your personality
Every personality has a lifestyle that suits it. Know the type of person you are. The things you like and you don't like. How far can you push yourself? When you know these things about yourself, you will be able to adopt the lifestyle that suits your person and identify with the type of social groups that suits your personality.

CHAPTER 31

What happens to you doesn't matter. How you handle the situations that you find yourself is what matters.

Life is beautiful. It doesn't mean everything is automatically fine. When they say life is beautiful, what it means is that life is such a drama and you and I, knows what happens in a drama. Series of events takes place in a drama. Some are favorable while some are not. There is the actor and the other casts, although some people acts the wicked script, but they are the one making the drama interesting.

Each time the actor makes progress, some people always want to bring him back and in that process, make the actor to work harder and smarter.

We won't have been smarter if there were no people who try to bring us down. Our strength comes from the fact that we are aware of the presence of the enemy. No one wants to go down. Everyone would like to be the last cat standing

Things That Happens to You
Everything that happens to you, no matter how little presents you with a hidden opportunity. Opportunities come in disguise. The event that happens to you gives you an opportunity of learning more and more of the things you need, to prepare you for the future.

Comfort zones don't prepare you for anything good. Instead they make it easier for your enemies to get you.

You should be happy when you face challenges and pray to God to show you the wisdom you need to tackle these challenges so you can learn your new lesson.

The events that are considered unfortunate come with higher amount of lessons to be learned.

If there was nothing like failure, people won't strive to be winners. The awareness of the presence of the negative makes us to even press harder towards the positive.

Zuckerberg, the founder of facebook was able to come up with the facebook idea as a result of the frustrated emotional situation he was in as at then. What happened to him was considered unfortunate but he turned it around.

Again I will say to you that the things that happens to you don't matter or the types of situation you are in but what matter is how you handle it.

Some musicians, who went through some horrible situation, put it into the records and that was what made their greatest success in the music industry.

What I am telling you is that all situations have a good side so you must always look for the good side of things. That's being positive

The right attitude
Having the right attitude towards situations is the key. Do tough situations make you stronger or brake you? Do they make you feel challenged or quitting? Do you see tough situations as temporary or permanent? Do you know that all problems need an answer? And are you aware answer providers are the inventors and geniuses that have improved man-kind?

Do you know that every tool you have used was an answer given by someone to a particular problem which is the usage of that technology? Which is your own problem that you want to give an answer to?

The beauty of life is the ability of being able to conquer even in the midst of all troubles. Dramas are so interesting because they contain a lot of or series of unfortunate events in which the actor was still able to conquer. In other words, the actor is a conqueror because he or she is able to build something real nice with the bricks thrown at him. Another question is: what if no bricks were thrown at the actor; would he had seen bricks to build with? Of course no, is the answer.

Another thing is that he could have simply thrown his bricks away or better still leave them exactly how they were thrown to him and he could have been a failure.

If there are no bricks being thrown at you, you have to make away or even beg people to start throwing some at you.

You need to face problems, you need to solve problems and the higher the problem, the higher the level of greatness hidden in it and so if you can find the solution to it, you would be that great.

CHAPTER 32

Disappointments, Regrets, Betrayals Are Part of Life's Ingredient That Helps in Preparing Us to Be Done.

Lets make the Preparation of a Soup a case Study

When preparing a soup, some ingredients are required to give the soup the expected taste. The type of ingredients applied defines the kind of soup being prepared as well.

We, as human being, we are the soup being prepared. All the pains you have gone through while attending primary school, high school and some colleges and other various professional examination bodies just to get a certificate were all part of your preparation.

The type of ingredient applied to the soup preparation defines its kind of soup. All the time you went to school, you are sure that you did not offer all the courses. You only offer some specific courses that geared towards the part of career line you were pursuing. That's the same way only some specific ingredients are applied to a soup.

All soup ingredients are not necessarily sweet such as pepper, salt etc but they compliment the taste of the soup. That's the same way all life ingredient are not necessarily sweet such as disappointments, regrets, betrayals etc but they make life complete.

What is Disappointment?

Disappointment can be defined as the sad feeling one gets as a result of something not being as good as they expected or an event not happening up to their expectation.

From the definition above, we can understand that when something is not up to our expectation, we feel disappointed.

The question I want to ask now is this: what if our own expectation for a particular thing was unreasonably too high and this thing now turns out to be moderate which is the best? We may still feel disappointed for the fact that we had gotten less than we expected; mean while we should be happy. Sometimes as humans, we don't know what we really need or want. Even when we know, we may not still know the right proportion. But usually nature has a way of making things happen the way they should and if this is less than our expectation, we feel disappointed.

What is Regret?

Regret is a period when one feel bad for some certain actions they have taken. This could come from doing some certain things and also from failing to do some certain things.

Usually in a time of regret, you wish to turn back the hands of time which is impossible.

To the one who is regretting, this period is an unfortunate one but most times, we make mistakes so we can learn to handle our future blessings a lot better.

In the past, one way or the other we must have pushed someone so special away and later on when we realized it, we wished to get that person back into our lives. The better side of these types of situation is that in the future when God gives you someone else special, you would have learned to be a better person.

Betrayal

It is hard to trust but we must always trust someone at every point in time. At worst, you would have to trust someone enough to review your will with them or else all of your properties would be lost when you die. But truly speaking, people had betrayed the trust being placed on them

Betrayal is part of life ingredient. We need it sometimes to fulfill what the scripture say about us. Jesus Christ knew Judas Iscariot was going to betray him and yet, he kept him within. He never made any plans of chasing him away for it had been written that the son of man shall be betrayed and Judas Iscariot made this scripture come to pass when he betrayed Christ.

Sometimes we need to be betrayed so we can make better choice of friends in the future.

No adventure, no lesson. The more that happen to us, the more lesson we learn.

CHAPTER 33

There Is No Problem That Will Come To You Without The Ability You Need To Solve It As Well.

There is a popular saying "More money, more problem", I believe it's true. "The higher your promotion, the bigger your responsibilities" "The more your affairs, the more your issues", "The more your fame, the more your freedom is limited or better still the more your controversies at times"

There is another saying that goes like this: "To whom much is given, much is expected. I still believe that the proportional system of tax is still the best; your taxing rate should be proportional to your level of income. Let there be a particular percentage tagged on one's income so that it will not look like a crime that somebody is being punished for earning so much or so little.

In principles of management, I learnt that authority should be equal with responsibility as stated by Henri Fayol. Imagine when one has more authority than his responsibilities; it would lead to so much abuse of power.

Also imagine when one has more responsibilities than authority; it would lead to inefficiency in the discharge of his duties. God will never give you a land to cultivate without the necessary tools that you need to cultivate it.

If you think your problem is bigger than you. Probably, it is because you have not discovered your God-given tools.

You need to find your tool room, go in and pick all the tools that you shall need and return back to the portion of land God has given to you and do a very nice job. So that when He comes to inspect in the evening, He would say to you "my son well-done".

There is this song by Mariah Carey that I love so much. The Title is: Hero. This song made me understand that the hero I need lies within me and all I have to do is search within me for the strength I need to carry on.

Believe you can handle it.
When a place is dark, everyone would be afraid to pass through it because of the fear that there might just be a big monster hiding in there. But when light shines through it, you find out that there had been noting in there.

You believe your problem is bigger than you because you haven't find how to tackle it or see through it to know its substance.

First you need to believe you can handle it. The moment you believe; the solution cells in your body are alerted to start finding solutions.

Give yourself courage
This is time for action. Once you believe you can handle it, attempt it. Trial by error is no sin. A lot of big problems had been solved through trials by error.

You can get courage by surrounding yourself with people, who believe in you, by reading books related to the nature of the problem.

CHAPTER 34

God Has Given Man The Ability To See The Visions Ahead But Not The Circumstances That Will Prepare Him For Its Actualization.

I want to let you know that there is no human being without a vision. God created us all with a particular mission to accomplish. So that our mission can be accomplished, God has given us the ability to see the visions. The purpose of the visions is to enable us to have an idea of our natural calling.

But there is one thing God does. God does not review to man directly, the circumstances that will prepare him for its actualization. No wonder the Holy Bible says that his ways are not the same with that of man.

When we are faced with some certain issues and then, we began to worry and complain, God just look at us and laugh because that circumstance we are complaining about carries with it some percentage of our preparation for the actualization of our purpose or mission.

Case Study: the School System.
Up till now many students still sees examination as a measure aimed at failing or demoting the student but rather examination are opportunities to be promoted.

I can still remember how many of my classmates back then, who usually develops fever during examination time. When they are taken to the hospital for medical checkup, the doctor sees nothing wrong with them order than examination panic. All this drama is simply because of the fear of examination.

No Examination, no Promotion

When you are tested and passed, then promotion comes. There must be some criteria, measurement or guideline that will prove your credibility before you are promoted.

That music group leader must have proven his or her credibility before being elected or appointed as the group leader. Same thing goes to the coach and others who are in the business of leading others. Out of all the eleven players in a football team, only one person wears the badge as the captain and that's because he had proven to posses more football skills than the others.

What about the politician-that senator, governor or even the president and many others who had to pass through screening before being allowed to become electoral candidates or appointment.

The Unforeseen Circumstances

The unforeseen circumstance is the examination that we pass through before accomplishing our vision, mission, purpose or goal. It could as well be referred to as the challenges being faced in the road to our success.

These challenges are not known to man ahead of time. If you have never been to a place, you will never know how it looks like exactly no matter all the descriptions that may be given. No wonder Gordons, a popular Nigerian comedian said that "there is difference between I was there and I shall be there".

If you try to calculate your risks before setting out on the road to your accomplishment, you shall surely miscalculate. I have come to understand that there is no such thing as calculated risk. A risk is already naturally calculated the way it is.

There are challenges or rather circumstances you will never be aware of until you start the journey.

No Time
Time keeps reading whether you are doing something productive or not. In short, the time waits for no one. So why not start your journey today. At least, hit the road today!!! Remember you don't know the exact circumstance that will prepare you to conquer so always tackle challenges with a positive mindset. Do not ever give up. Don't let it to even be an option because victory in your challenges will promote you instead and might just land you at your destination.

CHAPTER 35

Man Planeth But God Decides.

When I gained admission into the university for my first degree, I and my reading partner-Dandison read and studied so hard. We even went for TDB; a short formed of **Till Day Break**. We would prepare our studying materials and by 8: pm when other student are grooving, we are heading down to inside campus to spend the night reading in a classroom.

Soon, the examination period came; we wrote our best and waited anxiously for the results. To tell you the truth, the result for our first semester year one was beautiful.

When we got into 2nd semester of that same level, we applied the same technique we used in the previous semester. But then, when the results came out, I discovered something new. The courses where I had expected A(s), I got something less and where I had expected a lower grade, I got something more. That was when I knew that man plans but God decides what's final.

I knew at once after then, that the battle for a 1st class degree also have a spiritual side and it is even more of a spiritual warfare than physical.

Progress and Spirituality
➢ I believe in hard work;
➢ I believe in applying rules of success but then,
➢ I believe also in luck and spirituality.

Every progress you make have a spiritual connection. The spiritual actually controls the physical. You must understand that there is a particular spiritual body responsible for the success of any man. Mind you, this may be unknown to the person.

Everyone has an ancestral heritage and you cannot tell for sure all the various activities of your fore fathers. There must be something that your lineage had always believed in and worshipped. Those days our fore fathers did not only worship these gods, they also signed an agreement with these gods on behalf of their generation to come which you are among.

A good example of what I am trying to explain to you is the royal families. Right from ancient days, the royal families had always had something that they believe in and worshiped in exchange for protection and progress. So if you are an offspring, you are automatically connected to that covenant.

Like I said before, it is not everyone who is aware of the spiritual body that they are connected with; after all, not everyone is aware of their powers.

When something that should not happen to you starts to happen, it is a pure indication that there is a God somewhere who has a final say and that is it. This explains the reason why we can't find answers to some happenings in our lives.

The Titanic Ship

The titanic ship was referred to as indestructible but the titanic left queen town harbor and sank while en route to the United States on April 14, 1912.

From a human perspective, judging from the physical features of the ship, it was alright to refer to it as indestructible. The titanic was almost 900 feet long. It was specially built to tackle the challenges of the North Atlantic waves and other collisions that may occur.

The titanic was predicted to be able to stay afloat with 12 of its watertight compartment even when the remaining four watertight compartments are flooded.

The lesson learned was that it is God who decides. Man can only plan but it is left for God to decide what is final.

Back to the personal experience I shared with you earlier on, what I started doing is committing everything I do into God's hand. I do my best and then leave the rest for Him- God. I plan but still commit everything into his hands.

When I read and study, I tell Him to take control and when I write examinations, I also tell Him to take control as well. In everything I do, I always, tell him to take control and believe me, I have never complained and I will never complain about how he takes control in my life.

You can do the same, Go ahead with your plans, your arrangements and your strategies but commit everything into his hands knowing very well that He has a final say. God is the one who decides what is final.

CHAPTER 36

"God is God"

God is God everywhere all over the world. He is the same yesterday, today and forever. He changes not. He is not two. He is one.

God is Omnipotent. He has the power to do all things. He is omnipresent too; being everywhere at the same time.

We have all come from different background and that has added a lot of difference to our personalities and who we are. As a boy or girl from a Christian home, you are likely going to remain a Christian until you shall rest in peace. Same thing apply to the boy or girl who is born into a Muslim home. This goes a long way to affect their belief and general way of thinking. But the good news is that they both worship the same God although many believers are not aware of this. If only believers are more enlightened, there will be no need for religious wars.

This is more like a case whereby everybody wear clothes; be it silk, cotton, linen etc. they are all clothes and all over the world, we probably wear them for the same reasons just as we serve God for the same reasons but in different designs and pattern as a result of the influence of our diverse cultural background.

Between God and Satan
There are only two major actors in the world. They are: God and Satan.

God is the creator of all things while Satan is the devil. If you want to succeed in life, you will have to choose whose side you are in - God's side or the devil's side. There is no sitting on the fence. I bet you, it is even more dangerous to sit on the fence.

If you are on the side of God, you must know the following.

God is very Patient
It is not all prayers that God gives an instant answer. God's blessings always go through series of stages. By the time the blessing gets to us, we see it as a long awaited miracle.

You must learn to be patient with God. His timing is different from that of man; but His timing is also the best.

You must learn to follow God's Guidelines
God always gives guidelines. He could just tell you to rise, and move from where you are to the place that He will show you. All you have to do is obey his command even when you knoweth not where you goeth.

Everlasting Joy
God's blessings are everlasting and they give everlasting joy. It may take long to come but after it comes, it stays eternally.

If you are on Satan's side you must know the following.

Satan is sharply
When you go to Satan for wealth for instance, you get it immediately. No much challenges, but you will be making break through. It is more like easy come, easy go something. It happens like as if you are in a fast lane.

Your soul is traded

The most important thing in you is your soul. Devil does not ask for less. It is either your soul or no deal. The blood of your loved ones may serves as part of the deal. The main deal is your soul. Question is: what shall it profit a man to gain the whole world and loose his soul?

Short time Joy

Actually this is not real joy yet. It is for a very short time. The ending of those who get riches from the devil is always a very sad story. Since the devil has no time, he gives his disciples a very short time after which he welcomes them into hell for the real suffering.

There is a saying that "Nothing good comes easy" if you follow the side of God, you must have to plant your seeds and wait for harvest. Many people want to plant and reap immediately, some people don't want to plant; they just want to reap from anywhere. But if you allow me to advise you, be on the side of God.

CHAPTER 37

Big Income Doesn't Make One Rich But How You Control Your Expenditure Do.

When I was younger, I used to think that big income would make me rich but over the years, one of the things that I have learned is that big income would not make me rich and would not make you rich either. It wouldn't make us rich period!

I find out that the more I have, the more I spend and in no time, I am back to being broke. I also find out that just as I wasn't able to save when I had less, I couldn't have been able to save too even when I had more. I knew this was a serious problem and that I have to do something.

Truth 1s: I wasn't the only one having this kind of expenditure problem; a whole lot of us actually do. There are a whole lot of families who earn so big but they are still poor. They spend up to 80% of their credit worth, by the time they receive the monthly salary and pay up all their debts; they will only have 20% left for their pocket money. But because they think they are rich, they could start spending on some luxury things that may not really be necessary to them. By the time end of month is approaching, they must have wasted so much.

Some families do this for years. In some cases, without even having a house of their own and then they wait for pension money they will use to settle the mortgage. This is really bad.

Below are steps to overcoming the problem of excessive expenditure so you can be able to save and be rich.

Human wants are unlimited but resources are limited
In every second, we always want something. A man may decide in his heart not to buy another shoe until he's having problem with any of the ones he already had; but as soon as he sees another nice shoe in a show glass of a store, he makes another order especially when the money is there. This is our nature and we cannot change it but one thing, we should try to understand is that the resources to fulfill this wants are limited so we have to only try to fulfill the most pressing once. For instance, if I already have a nice three bed room bungalow where I can stay with my family, there will be no need for me to go and rent a duplex at the expense of my kids' school fees.

Calculate your Income
Calculate how much you earn. If you are a couple, calculate how much you both earn and get a net amount after subtracting your taxes. Knowing the net income that you earn would help you to know your financial stand and how you can try to push it up.

Identify your needs and your Expenses
Make a scale of preference. Arrange your needs according to their order of importance and try to satisfy these needs according to the scale that you have prepared. This will help you by reducing the chances of you, spending on things you don't really need.

Make out a budget from your scale of preference. Only spend on the things you budgeted for no matter how little they may be.

Whichever amount of money you budget for a particular need, you should divide it with 30 days in a month to know exactly how much you spend on it per-day.

Ensure your incomes is more than your expenses
What you need at this point is discipline. You need to learn how to stick to your budget so your expenses don't become more than your income. You would have to learn to be contented with the ones you have, while you patiently plan and save before buying that latest car that you admire.

Save
No matter how little you earn, you should always save. Open a savings account; do not link it to your credit card. Give yourself a target amount to accomplish at the end of the year. When the money in the saving account gets up to a certain amount, you can then withdraw from it; not for luxury consumption but for further investment.

I believe wealth is accumulation. The habit of saving over a long period of time is the surest way to wealth. The billionaire you know did not earn billions as salaries but they were able to save up to billions in order to become billionaires.

CHAPTER 38

Only Trust Those That Sees The Sorrow Behind Your Smile, The Love Behind Your Anger And The Reason Behind Your Silence.

Trust

This depends on the contexts it is being used but generally it means the belief that someone would not betray you or your interest.

As human beings we cannot escape issues with trust because in all our relationships, be it friendship, marital, business etc. trust have always played a key role. We have trusted people at one time or the other but they led us down and we vowed never to trust again based on that. I know you cannot trust anyone but you still have to trust someone at one point or the other.

This time around, you are not just going to trust someone; you will follow some guideline so betrayal of trust could be reduced to the minimal level. You won't have people break your heart every day. If you follow this guideline, you would be heartbroken ones in blue moon.

Have Few Friends

I am not saying know few people, what I am saying is that you should have fewer people that are your personal persons.

You are free to know everyone in the world; besides, it increases your chances of making a breakthrough but have one or two persons who understand you no matter the situation.

Trust those that see the sorrow behind your Smile
You and I both know that all cannot always be well with us. There are issues to tackle at every point. One stage to another, you know we just keep fighting in order to move forward but when you go out and greet someone and they asks you "how are you", the normal response is always "I'm fine". Most people will simply believe and go their way but few others would look at you deeply and tell you that you are not fine. These people, you can trust them because they can feel your pains and it is their wish to get you out of it.

Trust those that see the love behind your Anger
As a little child, you don't know what's right or wrong. Imagine a child jumping in a slippery place after which he falls and start to cry because he feels some hurts. The moment the mother sees that, she's angry and may in the process start yelling at the child for jumping in that slippery place. To other people, the woman is angry but in the real sense, that is love.

When the child felled, it was like she is the one who felled. There are those who truly loved us and are angry at us for so many things because they want us to get things right. These types of people take paracetamol (pain reliever) for our own headache. Sometimes we even suspect them to be having an ulterior motive but there is none. We can trust people like them.

Trust Those That Sees the Reason behind Your Silence
Sometimes we become very silent because we are overwhelmed. It could be either with joy or with sorrow. While we go through all this, very few people usually understands. Such is life and life is such, no matter what, we should always move on.

CHAPTER 39

If You Do Not Believe In Yourself First, Nobody Else Will Believe In You Either.

There are so many roads to greatness. You are the leader of any road that you take and so therefore you should lead by example. You are the standard that others look up to. The moment you let yourself down, others would let you down too. But when you keep on believing in yourself, others would have no choice than to believe in you also.

Believing In Oneself
Believing in oneself is simply the act of being convinced that you can do it or be it. Although it sounds simple to do, but there are processes you must follow. The following are guidelines.

Set your Goals
First and foremost you must have a goal that you feel the need to achieve. Your goal is a form of a new project that you would like to work on and after you are successful, you will feel fulfilled.

Build a strong Confidence in Yourself
In order to achieve this goal or dream, you need self-confidence. Self-confidence tells you that you can do it. It actually makes your dream achievable by making you to

visualize it more clearly and gives you, the courage to fight for it.

Take Constructive Criticisms but reject Destructive ones
There are two types of criticisms. The one aimed at constructing you for good and the other aimed at destroying you or discouraging you from trying to achieve your goals and dreams.

Mind you, most of the criticisms are aimed at destroying you. Very few criticisms are aimed at constructing you.

The difference between the two is that the constructive critics would criticize only a part of your aim and offer ways or options you can take to make it better but the destructive critics would usually disapprove the entire process, dream or goal. This form of critics tells you directly that your goal or dream is totally impossible. Do not ever accept this form of critics; they can only kill your dream.

Learn to Convince Others
A time will come when you would need others in order to move a step further. This is because no one has it all. In this stage, you would have to learn to convince others about your dreams, your goals etc you must be able to paint almost the exact picture of what you are seeing to them and be able to convince them that it is possible when they join forces with you. Most times it is not just by talking. People would like to see what level of success you have achieved on your own. So you must have done your homework properly and have some workings or structures to show as evidence of seriousness on your part (initiator).

Believe in God
After all your workings, you must realize that there is a supreme being who says let it be so or not. God has the final

say. You must believe and trust in him to bless every of your workings in order to be fruitful. Believing in God prevents your efforts from being fruitless.

Measure your level of success at every point
Always measure your level of success at every stage. It helps you to realize how far you have come so you can be more gingered in completing it. It is not every time that you should depend on the motivations from others, let your own level of progress motivates you and seeing how faster or nearer you are getting to your finish line even motivates you more.

Barrack Obama of the United State of America is an incredible example of a man who believed in himself. Though he is black, but yet he nurtured the dream of becoming the president of United States of America. Obama believed so much in himself that when people saw it, they had no choice than to support his dream. People of different races from all over the world believed in him because he believed in himself first.

Another example can be why you made an A in that course. You have seen people make an A in the course and so you believed that you too can make an A and when you put it into action, the A had no choice than to come your way.

CHAPTER 40

When Setting Up An Enterprise, Spend More Time To Draft Your Vision And Mission Statement Because They Are The Most Important.

A lot of firms think that they have a vision where as what they have is mission. Some firms do not even have at all. Your vision and mission statement must be in writing to serve as a reminder. Whatever thing a man does, he must have a vision and a mission or else there is no difference between him and a wanderer or fugitive. There has to be a form of direction or else the adventure becomes futile.

The Enterprise as a Being
By law, the enterprise is a being. It has right to sue and be sued. Like every other human being, the enterprise deserves to have a vision and mission that she is supposed to accomplish.

Vision
In a simple form, vision is the where we want to be. It is a futuristic statement stating where the company would like to be in a certain period of time or within a particular amount of years. It is usually a long period of years.

Mission
Mission statement focuses more on the purpose of the

enterprise. Mission, is about the thing that the enterprise hope to achieve.

Successful Enterprise
All the successful enterprises have a vision and a mission statement. Forget about the managerial skills, and the other resources such as humans, finances, materials etc, the first thing foremost is the vision and mission statement because that is what gives the direction to follow. It is the basis for decision making throughout the firm.

Microsoft is one of the most successful business enterprises of all times and she can proudly boast of a very good vision and mission statements. There are many other very good examples of enterprises with good vision and mission statement but I shall discuss Microsoft as a case study.

Microsoft Vision
It is: A personal computer in every home running Microsoft software.

The vision has guided Microsoft Corporation for years. It is the reason behind everything that they do, both consciously and sub-consciously. Although it sounded too tall a vision to achieve, decades later, it is almost a reality but they did not stop there. They continued to work hard.

Microsoft Mission
It is: To help people and business throughout the world realize their full potential.

This mission statement is in line with their vision statement by making their products relevant; their vision of being run by every personal computer is closed to being achieved.

Vision and mission is what gives direction of actions. If they are not there, it is hard to have a focus or direction. It must not necessarily be in an enterprise alone, in any endeavour you find yourself. If you plan to be successful, you must take out time to draft your vision and mission statement because they will guide your actions and enable you get closer to your dreams

CHAPTER 41

Circumstances Are The Rulers Of The Weak;
But They Are The Instrument Of The Wise.
- Samuel Glover

There are a lot of people out there who claims to be victims of circumstances. They give one excuse or the other, trying to explain why they couldn't make it. The truth is: every failure never runs dry of excuses or the reasons why they failed.

Save Yourself the Energy of Explaining to People all the Time.
Usually, failures spend their life time explaining the reasons why they never made it in every day of their life. Situation always prompts them to start explaining. It is a lifelong cross they would have to carry. The reason why they explain why they failed is because they feel empty and ashamed and in order to get people sympathy, they explain without even being asked. Instead of telling people how wicked your step mum or dad had been to you, or how unsupportive your parents are, why don't you device a way out. It is your future, your life and your everything. If you so much believe in the path that you have chosen and you have done your calculations right, why can't you be bold enough to prove to the whole world that you are unstoppable. This is not by shouting or you go about disrespecting everyone. If finance is the problem, it must not

come from your parents alone, look for other ways. If it is moral support, there must be someone who believes in you, identify that someone and move closer to the person.

When you start on your own, deprive yourself of so many other things of pressure, soon those that did not believe in you will starts to. Before you know it, they would become your biggest fans. But first, you need to understand that you are the leader of your path and you must prove yourself first before others can join you.

Failure is a Sin
Failure is a huge sin. I know some people don't believe in big and small sins; they say all sins are the same but the truth remains that: wounds have different level of deepness. You cannot compare a slap on the face with a murder case.

Failure is sin because you have no right to be a failure. There is a God somewhere who gave you everything that you may need and gave you life and then sent you to earth, not to go and be failure but to go and be victorious.

Imagine when you send your child to school and he comes back home with a 0/5 mark with the excuse that the class test was too hard. Yes may be the class test was too hard but there were other students who made 4/5, 5/5 despite the class test hardness.

There is nobody without Circumstances
Everyone faces circumstance because the road to success was never met to be smooth. The circumstances are not actually to make you fail but they are instrument meant to train and prepare you for your victory.

Usually people from the average or low class background sees people from the rich background as more privileged; but how? From far everything may look perfect but when you come closer to people, you realize that they have pains too. As a child from the low class background, you are very free to take any adventure but the child from the rich background faces so many limitations on the area of career path. Based on his family stand, there are some things he may want to do but his family forbids them because of their class.

No Road to Success is Smooth

If you are in a venture and it is going so smooth, you better think twice because it might just be the road to hell. There has to be some circumstances that will be threats to your survival. The greater your circumstances, the bigger your level of success if you apply the right attitude.

Not all things that Glitters is Gold

There is a wise saying that says: look before you leap. A lot of things glitter like Gold but very few are actually Gold. So you have no reason to envy others or think that they are more privileged than you. Check them out properly, a lot of them that you envy from afar actually envy you too.

CHAPTER 42

There Is No Moment Like The Present. The Man Who Will Not Execute His Resolution When They Are Fresh On Him Can Have No Hope From Them Afterward; For They Will Be Dissipated Lost, And Perished In The Hung And Scurry Of The World Or Sunk In The Slough Of Indolence.

- John Buroughs

There is this saying that "A journey of a thousand miles begins today". I totally agree with this. Although you may have not completed the journey today but with accumulation of yesterday and today's steps, it will be completed.

A lot of us have great dreams but somehow along the line depression sets in; after which we feel so exhausted and empty and the ability to continue to dream dies off. So many factors could be responsible for this. The following are a few important reasons.

Procrastination
This is simply the act of delaying things that you ought to do. When something is important, do it immediately at that time that you are suppose to do it because the moment you shift it forward, devil has a way of giving you more setback. Even if you happened to do it later, it might have been too late or you will pay more.

Lack of Discipline

A lot of people couldn't reach their peak because they lack discipline. Make up your mind to always do the right thing at the right time no matter what. If it is time to sleep, do not do anything else, go straight to sleep, if it is time to rehearse or practice, do not do anything else and over the years, you shall receive your great rewards.

Lack of Focus and Consistency

You need to at all times fix your eyes on your dream. No matter the issues you may be dealing with; always try to get in touch with your goals, your dreams etc. I know you may be saying now that Jay is not even aware that 1 am the one who pays my bills by myself, of course yes or may be no. But bills or no bills, if your dream is important to you, you can always save part of your time no matter how little in a day for it. This little effort each day amount to greater effort sometime in the future.

The other thing is **consistency**. Always be consistent. If you want to lose 5 pounds weight by the next 30days, you can start doing your work-out as from today, no matter how little the time you dedicate to it, just be consistent. Be regular at what you do.

What is the Way Forward?

John Buroughs, is telling you to start today, the race towards the execution of your resolution. When things are still very fresh in our mind, is the right time to start working. At this time, the motivation is usually very high and the will-power is stronger.

When you don't do something as at the time that it is fresh on the mind, laziness may set in and you may never be able to do it again.

The Present you are sure of but the Tomorrow, you are not sure of.
The present is the foundation. It gives you an opportunity to lay a very firm foundation upon which you can build in the future.

No one knows tomorrow except God. So it is much easier to do all that you have to do today and if by God's grace you see tomorrow, you continue from where you stopped today.

A lot of great people in the past didn't actually live to see their dream come true but others were able to continue building from where they stopped and helped them make their dream come. The most important thing is that they laid a good foundation at the time they were present. An example of such great man is martin Luther-King; his dream was that someday America will have a black president. He believed in the dream and did all that he can do while alive. Years later Barrack Obama became the first black U.S president.

CHAPTER 43

What I Gave, I Have
What I Spent, I Had
What I Kept, I Lost.
- Old Epitaph

A lot of people under-estimate the power of giving. They just aim at making all the money in the world without having any plans of giving. The people in this category see whatever they give out as a lost.
Although, we are all potential business men and women, we mustn't look at what we can get only all the time; some periods should be for giving back.

Who are those that should give?
Everyone should give, irrespective of your social status, age, sex, geographical location etc. "to give" is not compulsory but it is necessary.

No matter how bad you think your condition is, there is someone else who dreams to be like you.

Due to the introduction of currency into the economy, a lot of people now think that the barter system is outdated. Till today, most of the world major trades are still being carried out by the barter system. What I mean is – everyone can give because everyone has something to offer. It must not be necessarily in monetary form.

What I give, I have
Whatever a man sows; so shall he reap. Whatever you input determines your output. The farmer give his seeds to the ground and does all the necessary rituals, after sometime, called harvest time, he goes back and gets back what he gave out to the ground but this time around, he gets more than he actually gave.

Such is life. In the real sense, nothing given is lost. Do give more so you can get even more.

Invest into people's life; take their pain, just to make sure some people succeed. Companies are not the only institution to which people should invest in. You might not be appreciated up to your expectation but nature will be gathering your harvest for you to reap at the appointed time.

You do not need to be a good person to be able to give, besides, is there anyone that is good? All men justify the reasons for their action. So even the devil believes he is fair enough. But what I'm saying now is that "giving" should be everyone's part of life irrespective of who we are or where we are from.

"Giving" is the best investment. The reward can never be quantified. The reward of giving is always much more than expected. No wonder, even the devil encourage his members to give unto charity as well.

What I spent, I had
Whatever thing you used to get something else that is for personal consumption is regarded as something spent. But whatever thing that comes from you to another person for them to use for themselves is regarded as "giving". The bottom fact is that in both scenarios, something of value is going out of you but on the different grounds of reasons.

Sometimes life is not really about what you do but the reasons behind your actions. For instance, to disobey is neither bad nor good; it is the reason behind your action that will determine if disobedience is good or bad. When you are spending, what is your reason? Is it for your own self or someone else?

We should spend on ourselves as well but it shouldn't always be about us alone. We are blessed in order to put smiles on other people's face. The medical doctor was not trained to treat himself but others and make pains go away. What you spend on yourself for personal consumption, you can no longer have because it is an expense but what you spend to develop yourself or someone else is an investment.

Note that it is not necessarily all you spend on others that is an investment; some charities are waste unless being directed into improving someone's life.

What I kept, I lost

My grandmother used to tell me wealth is accumulation. What she meant is that I shouldn't spend all that I made in a day. I should be able to reserve some for the future and over a long period of time, becomes wealth.

I see nothing wrong with accumulating wealth for your next generation. The wrong that people usually indulge in is: not giving out some percentage of their wealth to the people who are currently in need. It is wrong to save up all your wealth for children unborn when there are children dying of hunger every day. If nobody helps the children or people who are currently in need of our resources, who would be the neighbors, teachers, etc of our unborn generation that we save up all our wealth for? In life, we should always try to strike the balance, save up wealth for your generation unborn if you have to but give out to those who are currently in need now and you shall be rewarded both here on earth and in heaven.

CHAPTER 44

No Man Could Be Ideally Successful Until He Has Found His Place. Like a Locomotive, He Is Strong On Track, But Weak Anywhere Else
- Orison Marden

Every person has their area of natural specialization. There is always an area for a particular person where he or she excels without really trying much. There are other areas where you work so hard and yet no much success but there is always a place where you are naturally specializing in.

Some people were so lucky to have been on the track where they belong right from early time. Such people finds themselves become geniuses in that area of specialization. Someone like Mariah Carey, Alicia Keys etc, has been on their track which is music, right from early days.

Michael Jackson and a whole lot of them who had started their career in a place where they belong have had tremendous success. Lionel Messi plays so well that some people believe he actually talks to the ball and the ball obeys him. It is more than just talent. Football is the area of his specialization, and he discovered this on time and was able to start early enough. But put Messi somewhere else, lets say music, acting, in the lab etc, he would not be able to do as much as he is doing in football because this other areas are not where he belong to.

Some people derailed for a while. After some years maybe a decade or more, they suddenly realize themselves and decided to make a U-turn and they lived a fulfilled life after.

It is not too late to make a U-turn no matter how much you have wasted, if you know that where you are is not where your passion lies, make that U-turn today and live your dreamed fulfilled life even though it is for a year, half a decade, a decade etc. you may be successful but not fulfilled simply because you are trying to be someone else.

Sometimes fathers could be very selfish. They just want their son to follow every footstep they want him to without checking for where the boy is naturally good at. For instance, a successful lawyer who has a chamber would want his son to read law at all cost so he can continue from where he would stop. This is very selfish of most fathers and very foolish of most children who obeyed.

A life career is a serious issue and should be treated seriously as well. When a child agrees to tread in his father's shoes against his own will, it is similar to living a life of impersonation. The God who gave you life would not be happy as well because He created you for another unique purpose and instead of trying to find out the way He is clearing for you, you derailed to impersonate someone else. John Mason says that you should ask yourself this question: if I try to be like him, who will be like me? If I'm not me, who will I be?

Finding your Place
Finding your place is not really hard if you are serious. All you have to do is to be sincere with yourself. It is not a case of teenagers whereby a guy is in love with a girl but does everything possible to denial it before his friends and then finally accepts when it is almost or too late. Be real to yourself. Only you know what your true passion is. You can also follow the following steps.

Childhood Hobbies

Go back to your days of childhood and ask yourself the things you liked doing naturally as a child, what you always told people you would like to become without thinking about it, the moment they ask you. Which subject were you naturally attracted to in your early school days and the sport you always liked to do during your school inter-house sports competitions.

Visit a Counselor

Take a visit to a good counselor who specializes on career counseling. You would be asked question, answer them all. The counselor would be able to tell you the industry that you belong to and two or three types of career that you may succeed in.

Seek Almighty God

God was the one who created you and it was for a reason and so he deposited in you all the instruments that you need to execute your purpose for living.

Seek God's face and allow him to speak to you while you listen. Invite him into your life and make him your coach and you will never be disappointed you did so.

You will only live life once and so why not live it to the fullest. The first step to living a fulfilled life is being on your right track so you can be the best in that lane.

CHAPTER 45

Don't Relax, Keep On Breaking Your Record and Setting a New One

To be a successful person, you have to be continuous in your record breaking and making. There is no much time to sit and relax or to celebrate. In the past centuries, battles were won as at the time of too much wine, food and celebration and as a result many kings lost their thrown.

Regretful mistakes are also made at the time of too much wine and merriment. The enemies always strike at the time the tension is low and when no one least expect an invasion.

After planning so well, working hard and strategizing and you eventually meets the target, I'm not saying you shouldn't be happy or shouldn't celebrate, but you should try not to allow the celebration take more time than necessary.

There are these movies whereby the actor is faced with the only option of fighting a monster that is trying to kill or hinder him from progressing, the moment he is able to dispose the monster, he would start to kiss and hug his girlfriend all in the name of celebration and suddenly the thought to-be dead monster wakes up again and hits him from the back. The movie you thought had almost come to an end would now be prolonged.

When relaxation is longer than necessary, the enemies takes advantage of it by striking. Usually the defense then, would be low and poor.

When you have achieved success, it is not a time to sit back and relax but a time when you need to work harder so you don't get beat down.

My Mum's mum used to tell me that buying the car isn't the problem but its maintenance. The same thing applies to success. If you had spent three (3) hours of your time daily to achieve it, you would probably spend more time to maintain it.

The time when one goes up, are the best because when you are already up, you need to work even harder to stay there or else you can only fall. Some people could say that if that is the case, then there is no need for them ever trying to go up but I say to you: every person is destined to be at the top of their various careers. So whether you like it or not, as long as you breathe, you are on a race and so why not just run harder so you can be the winner and you might just win it.

You have to do it and still be able to do it again and again. Artiste who made one hit album and they stopped are "stars" but the ones who did it all over again a couple of times are the "superstars". There is difference between a "star" and a "superstar". The difference is "consistency" on the part of the superstar.

Some others published once and they never tried it again when they could actually publish more.

Behind the Smiles

Every successful man should take this as a fact that everybody can't be happy for you and some people don't mind going extra mile to plot your downfall. This is usually very easy when you are still relaxing.

Among these people that smiles at you are some people who are praying and working day and night to see you fall. Another fact is that, they are present everywhere. Where two or more are gathered, there is a possibility of Judas Iscariot being present among them.

When you are too relax and celebrating, there are so many things that you may likely take for granted unconsciously. Celebration reduces your level of inquisitiveness

You need to work hard to do it and because you were able to do it, you can still do it again and again.

CHAPTER 46

The Best Investment So Far, So Good Is The One On Human Being.

Life is more about others than you; the candle spreads its light by reducing itself. As an income earner, more than sixty percent of your salary goes into your family and friends. You cannot be important if others do not acknowledge you. Your God-given talents are not for your personal consumption, they are given to you to use as instrument of light to help others. In the process, you are helping yourself also.

Even the rich man who piles up wealth for his next, next and next unborn generation, how much of his wealth has him been able to enjoy so far?

You make yourself great by making others great first. It is how much greatness that your teacher has been able to impact into you that reflect how great the teacher is as well.

A teacher cannot be seen as being great if his or her products are not great as well. All factors of life play a complementary role.

If you want to be great, then make it a principle that people will always be better than they were each time they meet you.

See People as God sees them

God sees people as they are supposed to be. It doesn't matter if they have reached the peak of their career or not.

If you were born a king, God starts to see you as a king even when you are still a crowned prince and yet to be king. Do not look at people present status and treat them according to that. Everyone has the potential to be better than they are as at present if appropriate steps are taken. So therefore do not look at a waiter as that common waiter because he might just be a restaurant owner by the next time you would see him again. I think Gordon Ramsey is a practical example of this. He grew from being the restaurant or kitchen boy to a group of restaurants owner. He is an authority in the restaurant world today.

When you see a singer who is good but not yet as recognized as the already famous ones, start to address him in that regard even when he is yet to hit a big record deal or be famous like the other ones. This show of believe in him can make him achieve his full potential and of course you know that the king maker is never forgotten.

As a teacher, you should understand that a lot of students who do badly in academics are not actually dull or dumb but they could be passing through a lot. It could be that all they needed from you is a little faith in them, a little sign of belief in them and their best could start to come out.

Criticize if you have to

Talent is not enough; one's attitude is needed to play an important role as well. There are people who have potentials to be something of admiration but their attitude is their own hindrance and stumbling block towards the achievement of their own goals. In this case when you meet people like this, you have a great role to play. Don't just be there with your mouth shut or trying to be in their good books. If you are sure of yourself, look for polite ways to let them know the problem they have. Pray for them also if you can.

We are creatures with red blood cells in our veins and so it is only natural that we should be humane.

In the process of trying to help, make sure you are very careful of your choice of words so your criticism could be constructive.

Spend Money if you have it
There are situations whereby the only thing needed from you is your financial support. So if therefore you have it, release it. That is what is called sowing of seed into another person's life because the seed will began to geminate and grow into something bigger than you thought.

The most successful companies are those that invest mostly into their employees. The greatest nations/countries are the ones that invest most into their citizen's life. This kind of investment has a way of increasing the patriotism of her citizens.

CHAPTER 47

We Are All Something but None of Us Is Everything

The entire world is like a whole system. This system comprises of different parts which function differently in order to keep the system going. The computer system for example comprises of the input devices, the processing device and the output devices. The combination of these devices makes the computer system complete and able to function effectively. The computer devices are interrelated. No one part can do everything but can all do something.

Same thing goes to human beings in the world. We have been made and blessed differently, every man according to his own area. By you and me doing a very good job in our various area of concentration, we make the world a better place to live. Without one of us little contribution, the whole system would be affected badly and that area makes an ugly picture.

What can you say about a mansion that is so beautiful but having none or very bad roofing? When we don't do our individual parts, that's how we make the world look like.

Interrelatedness
We must understand that whichever talent we have is not for ourselves only but meant to shine the light in a path to show others the way and that no matter how talented we may be, we are not everything. We need the cooperation of other talents as much as we feel they need ours too.

Just like in an organization which comprises of various departments; all the departments are indispensable. A production firm for instance, has the manufacturing, financing, accounting, human resource, research department etc. these departments all works together for the firm to be able to move forward.

The functions of these departments are interrelated in the sense that their performance is dependent upon one another for the entire firm to be able to achieve its goals.

Humility

"Humility is a Virtue", yes Indeed! Humility is a virtue. There are those that have it as part of their personality naturally.

But there are others who also have the opposite of it (pride) in abundance as part of their personality naturally.

I understand that temperament has a great role to play in our lives. It builds our personality up with combination of both strengths and weaknesses. So if you have pride as a natural trait, you need to know and accept it. It will be a great way to start gradually, you could be able to put away pride and replace it with humility.

For self development and success, humility is a must-have feature. True great people have humility and very little of pride. At each point, they feel that they have not done well enough. There is a drive in them to always be better.

You must value others and treat all as something. The truth is, "no man is nothing, but are all something".

Humility also attracts favor to those that have it. When you have humility, people naturally want to support you.

I see no need for pride because no matter what you think you've got, there is someone else whose own is starting from where your own ends.

Feel important but not at the expense of others. So you can benefit more from them.

CHAPTER 48

You Can Only Make It By His Grace

According to Rev. Canon Saturday T. Nbete, "grace is something that God gives to his children in order to compensate for their deficiencies. A lot of men and women have clinched top positions that in the eyes of men and women, they do not qualify to occupy but by simply the grace of God. But whether they are qualified or not, the bottom line is that the position has been occupied by them.

When the grace of the lord puts you in high places, men begins to think that you belong to a secret cult. Truth is: you belong to the cult of the Most High God.

I have witness a lot of cases whereby the most qualified looses the race to the less qualified. After a while I was made to accept that it is not how hard or smart you work only, but simply by the grace of God. There just has to be a thing working for you and most importantly let it be the one that comes from the Most High God.

The Royal Kingdom as a Case Study
How many first sons actually took over the royal kingship from their father? How many do you know? Go and check history of the time before Christ (BC) and the time after the death of Christ (AD), you would find out that somehow most of the first sons always missed it.

Lets go to the holy Bible. In the book of 1Samuel 10:1-27 the Israelites asked God for a king and their first king was chosen from the 12th Tribe of Benjamin in the person of, Saul. Israel is made up of twelve (12) tribes. The twelve (12) tribes are the generation of Jacobs twelve (12) sons and Benjamin being the 12th son and the youngest, but the first king of Israel was chosen from here and from amongst his clan.

This is an evidence of grace that the first king of Israel was chosen from the clan of the youngest tribe and not the oldest.

Saul had a son, Jonathan who is supposed to be king after him but because of the grace of the lord upon David, he became the next king of Israel.

Again, let me remind you also that king David was the youngest son of Jesse. The first son, Eliab who looked most qualified in the eyes of men was not chosen.

David went on to become 2nd king of Israel. After his reign, Solomon who is not the first son of King David took over from him because he found grace in thy Lord's sight.

Grace... Unmerited Favor

Today, grace is being referred to as unmerited favor by many. The rate at which some people are progressive makes it looks so obvious that a spiritual force is working for them but you know that it is simply grace.

Some singers had won more prestigious award and gotten more honor not because they were actually the best, some football players had more recognition not because they were the best in the team but it just happened that the grace of God is with them. You may be the most hardworking and available and still miss your momentum if you are not there at the right time with the right people or if you do not have His grace.

Let us therefore come boldly unto the throne of grace, that we may obtain mercy, and find grace to help in time of need. Hebrew 4:16 (KJV)

Hard work cannot do everything for you
Hard work may bring you a woman or a man to marry but certainly not a wife or a husband.

Hard work may get you a bed but not a sleep. Hard work may get you drugs and give you access to the best physicians but not a good health, hard work would give you a house but not a home or family.

Grace is like a spiritual strategy. It compensates for the lacks that we were supposed to suffer from.

How to Obtain Grace
There is no special way to get grace, even before now, you have been getting it unknowingly. It is by his grace that you have lived up to this hour and also by his grace you are reading this book now. There is just one thing you need to do hence forth.

Keep believing in His Grace and Him even as you put your best into your workings, know and believe in your heart that you are only moving forward because of his grace upon you.

CHAPTER 49

The More You Grow, The More Clean Your Hands Should Become.

Success has its own announcement. A successful man is like a man who had tied bells to his waist, and when he is walking, the bells announces his presence.

Your workings may be in the secret but your success is always public. You do not need to tell everybody what has happen, the few you have told is enough.

A Celebrity
A successful man is like a celebrity. When you are successful, you become a celebrated person according to your level of success. Celebrities are role models or at least, are supposed to be role-models. As a celebrity, you only get to know a fraction of the people that knows you. There would be a lot of younger fellows who would be looking up to you for a source of inspiration to themselves.

As a celebrity, you would agree with me that your private life is being looked into and people always want to judge your every single decisions.

Be Clean Deep Down
The more you grow, the more celebrated you would become and the cleaner you should be. This is because it is not only about you anymore.

Now that you have the power to spark up a change, which one are you going to do? Positive or negative? Let the change start from you, make a conscious effort to eliminate some of your bad habits and give more financial aides, psychological, emotional support and more. That way, you are sparking up a positive change because you are a mirror and people are looking at you.

Secret Enemies
In the midst of those that would be celebrating you, are also your enemies. I call this type of people situational enemies because they become your enemies the moment you go higher and become your friends, the moment you come down but your interest is in what is important, not theirs.

Some of these situational enemies are harmless and others are harmful. The harmful ones would always have a lot for you. The question is: how do you win?

The answer is simple: He, who goes to equity, must go with clean hands meaning that if your hands are not clean, equity cannot save you. The Holy Bible also made us understand that the only way to have victory over evil is by staying clean.

Many things fight for you when you are clean even without you noticing it. Learn to say sorry to those you have been unfair to. Do not intentionally hurt people. Avoid things that would bring issues the best possible way you can so you don't waste your energy unnecessarily. By this way, you can have all the time to remain focus and stay clean.

CHAPTER 50

Always Forgive Those That Trespass Against You.

Irrespective of the religion that you belong to, forgiving those who trespass against you, is mandatory. You should always forgive those that trespass against you.

I mean not in a year, or decade time but almost immediately. Learn to forgive as soon as you can. Even before the person apologizes, start preparing your mind to forgive.

I know you may say "it is easier said than done" yes, that is true but do not forget "that nothing good comes easy either. To forgive is good and so it would be a little hard to do but the good news is that no matter how deep somebody had hurt you, you can always forgive if you really want to.

Do To Others As You Want Them to Do To You

This is a rule; you may call it a principle, an ideology, a guideline, a fact etc but it pertains to every human being irrespective of our background and religion.

If you want to be forgiven, then you must forgive also.

If you want to be loved, you must love first. If you want to be supported, you must support others first.

If you want to be given, you must give also and so on and on. This is life.

As we go about our daily routine, we step on toes sometimes. Some of us do not deserve the air we breathe right now but because somebody was able to forgive us, we now have another chance.

Trespassing Is Inevitable
Trespassing against one another is inevitable in our daily lives. So the best way to go about things that we do not have the power to stop is to manage them. The best way to manage trespasses against us is forgiveness.

To Forgive Is For Your Own Good
To forgive is for your own good. You benefit more than even the person that you have forgiven.

Below are the things that happen when you forgive.
- You would become at peace before God and Man
- Your spirit is released from captivity.
- You would become free from the burden of the past.
- You would be able to concentrate on the present and future.
- You would become more successful.

You Would Become At Peace Before God And Man
In the eyes of God, you now deserve to receive some favors. Favor that ordinarily you are not entitled to, but because you have forgiven all those that trespassed against you, it now makes you have a kind of a clean slate and if God is looking for people to bless or to promote, you are short listed automatically.

Before man, you stand the same chances of even being forgiven by others as well.

Your Spirit Is Released From Captivity
When somebody trespasses against you and you refuse to forgive, you and the person's spirit remains in that pit

(captivity). Both of you would keep struggling in it and that is not healthy for you spiritually and physically.

You Would Become Free From The Burdens Of The Past
Nobody moves on until they forgive. Forgiveness is the key that gives you the energy to let go.

As long as you have refuse to forgive, your wounds will always be fresh and every second, you are being reminded of the wrongs being done to you. You cannot be truly happy when you carry on like that. Although you may not notice it quick, you would be getting older than your age. Another danger of unforgiveness is that the cells in your body that are responsible for your happiness starts to die out and before you know it, your immune system is getting weak also. Your doctor can elaborate more on this.

You Would Be Able To Concentrate on the Present and Future
Because you have forgiven, your energy is reserved. You would have all the energy you need to concentrate on your present and future. Your decisions will become sounder. Mentally, psychological and physically you are alright. Your friends and loved ones can now really be happy by your side because the poison is gone out of you.

You Would Become More Successful
Now that you think clearer, act wiser, definitely you would become more successful. Your decisions are free from sentiments and also, you are being guided by the self-will to do the right thing.

To forgive have more benefits than the ones we have just discussed. So be the type of man who is easy going, not because he doesn't get offended but because he has refused to be offended.

CHAPTER 51

I Have Found Out That If You Love Life, Life Will Love You Back
-Arthur Rubinstein

We want to be successful and definitely in this life, not in Pluto, Mars, Jupiter or in some other planet but in this life. The life here refers to this earth.

One deep secret of successful people is loving life the way it is and in return, life loves them back.

How Can I love Life
You can love life by accepting life. Life is not bed of roses, it operates by some principles that you must learn to obey.

Nothing Good Comes Easy
It is a popular phrase and at one time or the other, we have had a situation that seemed to explain this but very few of us had really sat down to analyze the phrase.

Imagine a meal that took you 30-45 minutes to prepare is being eaten all up in 5 minutes.

Imagine a whole month rehearsal for a show; finally performance is only in 5 minutes.

Imagine all the days of courting, wedding is only a day. And the list goes on and on. Everything around us seemed to remind us that in life, "nothing good comes easy".

Now that you have known this fact about life, the right attitude is to accept it that way, you are loving life and things could begin to be easier for you.

The Light Will Not Always Be Green
Another principle of life is that "the light will not always be green". Sometimes the light has to be red for you so it can be green for others. You must acknowledge this fact and accept it so you don't get mad or ask questions unnecessarily.

Whenever the light is not green for you, it is an opportunity for you to follow someone else's lead, an opportunity for you to act calm-that is, keeping a low profile and patiently waiting for the green lights to turn towards you.
Every situation has its Boss. This means that there is no one Boss for all situations. In every situation, you should be able to know who the Boss is. If you happened not to be the one pulling the strings, be loyal and that way you would be free from being bruised. "Give honor to whoever honor is due" is a very wise phrase. I have heard this since I could barely know what life is all about but as time went on, I began to understand it.

Some people are ready to take their honor by force but you will make life more loving if you just give honor to those that it is due so that your due honor can be given to you as well.

To Love Life
To love life is simply appreciating, the good and the bad, the beautiful and the ugly, the sweet and the bitter etc. Basically to love life is to accept its both sides and naturally life will love you back by making you successful and happy.

CHAPTER 52

The Greatest Pleasure of Life Is Love
- Euripides

Many of us would have said this many times but how many of us had sat down to analyze what it truly means? When I look around me, the things that I do, the people around me do, both the ones that affect me negatively, positively are as a result of feelings.

Our hearts is being controlled by love. All I am trying to say is that love is the greatest asset that one can ever have. The absence of love in a man's heart turns him into a monster while the presence of love in his heart turns him into an angel in a human form. The deep reason behind our hustle and the chase after our dreams should be connected with love somehow. It may be indirectly or directly.

There is a secret desire nurtured by every individual and that desired is for their parents and loved ones to be proud of them. You may have quarreled with them but the desire to still make them to be proud of you should always be there.

In a situation where the loved one is gone, we still wish that they are proud of us wherever they are.

Who do you celebrate with?
We are nothing if there is no body to celebrate with during the time of major achievement in our lives. There must be someone that you would really like to be with.

Achievements are good but love is Greater.
Dreams are good but if there is no love in our lives, there won't be a conducive environment for the achievements. Some people had killed directly or indirectly just to achieve something. The question now is where is the love? Imagine a world where only you live in, would it matter if you were the best singer, the best writer or the president of United State of America? So why do you still spill blood just to achieve something. Remember those you've killed are other people loved ones.

Success is Internal Peace in the Midst of your Achievements.
If you have a favorite soup and love is its major ingredient, without love present in the soup, would the soup still be sweet? When you follow the right way to achieve your goals, there is an internal peace that comes with it. This is what is referred to as true success.

To have Success is Different from to Achieve
Many people have achieved but they don't have success.
    If you can look at your achievement and be proud that you achieved them in an almost faith, then you are a success. But there is no way you will achieve in an almost faith without love in your heart.

Achieving True Success.
Fill your heart with love. As you go about the race, you should only hurt unintentionally. Do not look desperate by making your achievements look effortlessly and become a success in any level.

CHAPTER 53

In Every Situation, Recognize Who The Boss Is.

Life is full of situations. Many different situations take place in a second. Call it events, call it happenings, call it issues, call it problems, call it occasions, call it whatever name you want to call it, the bottom line is that an action is taking place. There can't be two captains in a ship. Even if there is, one is first amongst equals.

Know when you are the Boss
Knowing when you are the boss is not hard. If the final decision rest with you, that makes you the boss of the situation. It means therefore you are free to put on your boss hat after all; it is what you decide finally that will hold waters.

Know when you are not the Boss
Knowing when you are not the Boss is even easier but harder to accept. Some people do not just want to accept that their decision holds no weight in a particular situation. May be they have been too used to having the final say in other matters or they are just like that.

Arrogance won't take you anywhere.
Some people always want to be boss in all situations but you must learn that in life, you can't be boss in all situations. If you happen not to be the boss in a particular situation, the faster

you accept it, the better for you. When you are arrogant, you drive away sympathy from you; you make the boss angry and get even more bruised.

When you are arrogant, you are your own stumbling block to your open doors. The Boss will become more alert at you and would watch out for you more. Your chances of rising becomes slimmer.

It is About Being Successful Right?
If playing cool would make you successful, why not do it?

In the corporate environment, some people have enjoyed tremendous promotions; just because they realized when to play cool and when not to play cool.

Avoid Unnecessary Enemies as much as you can
If you really want to keep on climbing your ladder of success, too many enemies are not good for you. I have never seen a one man army and I believe it doesn't exist. As much as you want to protect your interest, subtle ways are best. Subtle ways may take long time of planning and waiting but at the end success is yours.

Let me give an illustration to help you understand properly.

The president and the doctor
The president is the number one citizen of a country. All bows to him but not all the time because we do have different situations.

Let's assume the president is sick and he is taken to the health centre to see the doctor. Because he is the president, he will be given a preferential treatment but the truth remains that as long as the president's treatment is concerned, the doctor is the boss. The doctor tells him to lie and he lies, sit and he sits, all in the name of trying to carry out a check up on him.

After then the doctor would recommend some drugs and measures the president needs to adhere to in order to be well again.

But imagine that the president is arrogant and refuses to follow the doctor's advice; won't that be at his detriment? The president would be blocking his own chances of recovery. This is exactly what happens when we claim to be boss in a situation that we are not boss.

CHAPTER 54

Play Loyalty

This is one simple thing but very hard for many to do. Everybody demands it from others but how many of us give it to those that need it from us?

Loyalty and Discipleship
Discipleship is the first step; a step deeper is called loyalty. When you follow somebody and keep to the person's instruction or way of doing this, you are a disciple of that person. When you are consistent with what you do and it's from your heart, now that's loyalty.

Nothing is New under the Moon and the Sun.
There is no path that you shall take that is entirely new. What we have is the mix up of different element in order to have something new. When Afro-pop music was originated, people said it was unique and new but it didn't come with its own brand of instrument? The same instrument used for pop, R&B and other music were combined to produce the genre we now call Afro-pop. So nothing is entirely new. What this means is that you must tap from an already existing body of knowledge or a form of foundation that had already been laid before. For you to be able to tap from an existing structure, you need to play loyalty.

Everyone needs someone to carry them along in their various chosen line of career. You will need to come out of your comfort zone to find this people. When you have found the one that you need to carry you along, your own is to be loyal.

There have been so many cases of young upcoming artiste playing loyalty to a big name in the music industry. As we all know, one day is always one day. The young man is given a chance to contribute to production and you will see him blowing up like a star. The lesson to be learned here is that his loyalty was required first before his talent.

Give Honor to the Person It is due

To be successful, you need to give honor to the person it is due. There are people, who had paved the way for you, when you meet them, honor them. Your own time is coming when people will honor you too because you have paved the way for them also.

Some time you need to honor them for more ways to be paved for you.

You Need Humility

They say humility is a virtue. You need it to be able to play loyalty. Humility has a way of drawing people to you; people that can help you and to make you more successful. People are always watching and are ready to fight for you when you are humble.

You Need Recommendation

Recommendation is another powerful tool you need in your ladder of success. Actually, recommendation is the son of loyalty. From being loyal, you will get to be recommended. Most successful people today are products of recommendations. Many politicians are appointed through recommendations. People have gotten jobs through recommendation. Business men and women know the power of recommendation. As a matter of fact, that's what they use in their everyday business. When you are recommended, you are been given a fresh chance and then it takes your capability to move on from there. But are you aware that there are a lot of people who are more capable but they don't just get the chance at all. You are punishing yourself when you always have to struggle with the multitude. All you need to do is to be loyal to somebody and get that person to recommend you.

CHAPTER 55

Influence Directly or Indirectly, Which Ever Ways, Make Sure You Are Influencing.

Do not just sit down there and let people dictate what happens to you. Very few people would have your own interest at heart. In fact you are the only one that can fight for your best interests. Others would always fight theirs before yours. When you sit down there and do nothing, others apportion the best areas to themselves and whichever crap remaining becomes your own portion. So you must always strive to influence in order to get your expected result.

Influencing Directly
Sometimes the most effective way is for you to do it directly not through others but yourself. There are times that what you truly want cannot be placed in exact words. Lets use the political environment for an example.

Sponsoring Yourself for a Post
This is a direct way of influencing. If you were to contest for the presidency, only you see the picture of your dream country. No matter how much you try to explain it with words, people can only have an idea but not that vivid picture that you yourself sees only. No wonder political candidates who truly have vision never really get tired of telling in campaigns and debates. They keep on looking for words to explain the picture

that they have in mind. In cases like this, influencing directly is the best as long as you are convenient and eligible enough to contest.

Influencing Indirectly
Sometimes you may be too busy to be the one in a position to influence things directly. It could be that you are not eligible enough but that doesn't mean its over. You have the option of influencing indirectly by sponsoring your interest. There are so many ways to sponsor. It could be in finances, morally and other wise, get somebody to fill in the post; somebody who would or listens to you.

This is mostly practiced by associations, corporate bodies, business moguls, politicians, countries etc. There are so many instances I can give especially in the areas of international politics whereby bigger countries sponsor smaller counties for a post in order for them to manipulate these counties later on for their own interests but I am sure with the picture of what I've been trying to paint, you now understand what I mean.

Politics is everywhere
Politics is a game of interest and all human beings acts based on interest so I laugh when people come out to say that they are not politicians. We might not all be professional politician but we all are, as long as there is always something to influence at every level. At every level could be in the church, mosque, family, friendship etc.

In the family for instance, the son may want a particular assistance from his father but knowing very well he cannot get it from the father if he should request directly, he may decide to use his mother or someone else whom the father will likely listen to. What do you call that? That is politics.

Influence for the Right Reasons

Whether directly or indirectly, makes sure you are influencing but influence only for the right reasons or else it back fires. Things done with ulterior motives always have a way of snapping back at us. So therefore, in as much as we need to influence situation in our daily lives, let it not be at the detriment of others. If you had to kill a person to be rich, that is not success. But if someone had to die a death that is not of your own doing in order for you to be rich that could be success.

CHAPTER 56

Running Too Fast Does Not Guarantee That You Will Get To Your Destination.

In running too fast, you may get to your destination but the chances are slimmer. It is not a mystery why the chances are slimmer. After all do you spot bumps easily when you speed above 160? In the past, people had run very fast and they got to their destination. Presently, there are people running too fast and they will get to their destination surely.

It is not as if you wouldn't get to your destination if you run too fast, the
 emphasis here is on how much guarantee that you would get to your destination. For instance when you have a statistics that says that only about 5% (five percent) of those who run too fast actually got to their destination; do you still need a prophet to tell you that running too fast is a bad idea.

The more painful one is when people start very well; moving at a steady average pace and just when they are almost getting to their destination, they began to run too fast and eventually an accident comes to stop them. The story becomes sadder. If we look around us, we would see a typical example of people like that. There are people that made money too quick and when they got to the time of their life when they needed the money the most, the money stop coming quickly too. People like that spends, most of their time reminiscing the good old days. The question is: Is your today not supposed to be better than your yesterday? And your tomorrow better than your today?

When driving too fast
Let us take a look at when driving too fast, having those real life factors in mind such as
a. Other road users
b. Possibility of bumps in some part of the road
c. Possible sharp turns in your lane etc.

When you are driving on a high speed or too fast, things happen in a second. For instance, when you have another motorist coming from behind you, you will need to adjust your steering, the same goes when you have one coming from front. Traffic lights are there for you to interpret immediately and also obey. Unexpected bumps at one side of the road that you will need to avoid or it could cause your car to summersault, these are factors you consider before you start speeding.

There are so much more factor while driving that needs to always be considered and within a very short time.

Speed will reduce the amount of available time needed to avoid an accident.

Speed makes it very possible for an accident to take place.

When an accident takes place, speed makes it even more fatal. The bottom line of this whole accident is that you are prevented from getting to your destination.

Move at your Pace
When you move faster than your shadows; that is running too fast. Moving at your pace simply means moving at your own capacity. When you run too fast, you exhaust resources met for future use. It is like wearing an oversize shoe when you are yet to grow to fit into the shoes.

Running too fast is exactly how it is like when you are driving too fast.

Resources you have now are for your concurrent race, when you run too fast, it is like over stretching your resources. Everybody have their own speed limit. Know yours and try to stick with it so you don't crash before you get to your destination.

Undue Double Promotion
Back then in school, I used to be in a class where some of my classmates were given undue double promotion. The promotion is undue because they were not ripe or qualified for it but they were rushed by their parents; that was a clear example of running too fast.

By the next section resumption, these unduly promoted students resumed their new higher classes. At first, it felt good especially when you look at your former classmates and you are now their senior. They were actually fooled to believe that they were one step higher than us-their former classmates but no. Soon later, the dangers of running too fast began to dance around them. They struggled to get to the final class where they need to take the final high school examination that will qualify them entry into any of the highly reputable universities in the country. But that was when the problem became even bigger. Some of them made very poor grade that couldn't get them admission in a reputable university and others had to go back and take extra curriculum classes in order to take the final examination and make good grades but that was in the following year. At the end, they got slowed down at the time they needed to move. It is like when you are over speeding and the police blow siren on you, you would finally spend even more of the time that you were trying to save over speeding.

Handling too Many Project at the Same Time
This is another form of running too fast. Some people could be handling too many projects at the same time and worst of it is that, these projects may even be unrelated. For instance, a man who is an actor, a singer and a model at the same time could cope because his projects seems to be related or in the same industry. When you have too many projects to handle at the same time, there is a way out.

Delegate Responsibility
Learn the act of delegating responsibilities. Every manager who wants to be successful should learn how to delegate responsibilities to subordinate. The rule is simple. Always make sure that when you delegate, responsibility equals Authority or else there would be an abuse of the one that is more.

If you do not want to delegate, then you should put some of your projects on hold to enable you enough time to focus on the other ones. You will be able to give your best at the end of the day; you will do a better job.

CHAPTER 57

Enter Action with Boldness

Many have big dreams but very few are bold enough to start. Some people had been waiting for the right time to start since the past four decades and up till now, there is no sign of them starting. When you approach them, they have ten thousand excuses to give and the most common one would be; "I'm waiting for the right time". The truth is there is no 100 percent best times to start or do anything. All you need is to adjust some few things and start without even having all the resources that you need.

Most people have had to stay in rented house all the days of their life, not because they didn't earn enough to own their own house but because they were waiting to save up the complete amount for their dream house. The amount never really got completed, with the effect of inflation, the amount keeps rising and then later, retirement and other pressing needs came up.

Many that owns their houses today before their retirement didn't achieve that because they had a bigger pay check then, it was just simply an art of boldness. They planned and strategized and enter into action with boldness. They started with the amount of money they had spread on mortgage over the years and in a matter of years later, became their own landlord.

Fear and timidity are brothers and they do not ever accept the truth. A man who has been unable to take a bold action into achieving a particular thing simply because he is fearful or timid would never accept this as his reasons. Fearful and timid people always pretend that they care about others. They will always tell you that the reason they couldn't start is because of John. If it is not John, it would be Peter. A man who is afraid to go into the world and make a mark for himself would stick to his parents with the excuse that he loves his family so much that he can't leave them. Actually, if he loves his family so much, he would leave them and go into the world to clear the way for them to walk through. The following are facts that you should adhere to in order to be bold and successful.

The Road to Success is Personal
It is usually timid people that wait on others. If anybody is not ready at anytime, whereas you are, move on; there is a popular saying that time waits for no one. While then, do you have to waste precious time waiting for others?

In the past I have planned with some friends to set up a business venture. We planned all the way and all the decision was jointly made so nobody was forced to be part. I brought out my money and I began to lay foundation and the so-called partners to-be were there when I started to finance the plans we jointly made but to my amazement, when it got to their turn to do something, they backed out with domestic excuses. Plans were abandoned and my money went down the drain. I picked myself back together and I went into something else that I can do myself without begging for partners who will disappoint me at the last minute.

If you have something tangible to work on, go about it without waiting for others. Later some others would realize themselves and come and join you. But first you need to display that boldness. The world admires boldness but no one admires timidity.

Never Attempt until you are sure
Never go into an action with half boldness. If not you would wish that you never started at all. Going into an action with half boldness would enable you to start but become stranded in the middle. It would raise people expectation and when they expect you to do more, you would become a disappointment. It is like travelling with half tank of fuel in your car, assuming that there are fuel stations along your route. And then your car gets to the middle of the journey and breaks down, you would wish you never started the journey at the first place. In as much as you don't need everything to be ready to set out, but you should know the non-negotiable needs and make sure you satisfy them before setting out. For a man who wants to travel with a car, an air conditioner or a nice music player in the car would not be a bad idea but a full tank of fuel and a spare tire are non-negotiable.

Bravery is needed to pass Through the Storm
The obstacles that can break or make you are not placed in the beginning of a journey. They come much more lately. The ending of the day started with the evening and it gets darker slowly; by midnight, it's darkest and if you survive through the mid night, the next day time becomes your celebration. If you had used courage to start, you would need more courage to finish.

Prepare for the storm in advance. You started with bravery; you need more of it much later when the storm would start to blow. The reason why most people starts very well but later fail is that they seemed to have used all their weapons in the beginning and having less weapons to fight in the middle when the battle gets tougher.

Enlarge Your Dreams as Possible
Timid people are sometimes afraid to dream big. They are their own enemies. They tell themselves they cannot even before the world joins them in telling them they cannot. It is normal to dream big and if a voice inside of you should ask you; "is that not too outrageous"? Are you that good enough to achieve that? But with the spirit of boldness, you would be able to shout that voice down. Funny enough, a dream that you feel is too large for you is even the least of another man's dream so do not limit yourself because you have nothing to lose. You lose a whole lot when you limit yourself. As long as you can dream it, you can think it; there is a possibility that it can be realized.

Making your dream outrageous has more benefits than making them moderate. It is not every time you make things moderate. If you have dreamed to be president and you ended up being a governor, have you not gained? But if you had made your dream moderate by dreaming to become a permanent secretary and you ended up being just a senior civil servant, have you not in a way reduced your level of achievement?

An undergraduate student wanted a second class upper degree but deliberately aimed at first class so that at worst; he would get the one that he had wanted. It would have still been good if he had eventually gotten a first class. The strategy was a win-win.

It is About You Not Others
Your success is about you, not others. After God you should consider yourself next unless in a situation whereby you are not in that same race. What others have to think or say is not your business. You know your goals and it is paramount for you to achieve them especially when they are not inimical to the interest or growth of the state. If you are to go on a journey and everything you would need during the journey is ready with

you, embark on it not minding what others have to say. People will always talk no matter what.

Constructive criticism aims at bringing out the best in you and so you should know when someone offers you one. There are people who will always talk whether you are right or not. Ignore these set of people completely because they have no positive contribution. When you know the right way, do everything possible to follow it.

e
—

CHAPTER 58

The Crowd Is Foolish but the Individual Is Wise

Year one student in the university often moves in crowd. They are all in a new environment and so they look up to each other. At the early time you would find people of uncommon interest and behavior moving together or rather following themselves but with time, they will now begin to understand and know the people who shares similar aspiration with them. At this stage, the crowd movement would begin to split into dyads (group of two people). You would agree with me that as at the early stage when year one students moved in crowd, they did some foolish things that ordinarily they wouldn't have done if they were alone.

A group of fresh students were in a place thought to be their lecture venue but were unsure of the venue. After a while, one of them stood up and began to go, the rest saw him and began to follow him. They followed him till the point that one of them asked him where he was going. That was when he now replied that he was going to urinate.

Somebody was going to urinate and a whole lot of people started following him because they were a crowd. When crowd of boys goes to the club, even the one with the least power or who is naturally quiet may just become the most troublesome. There is one thing about crowd mentality; it does not give one enough space to reason properly and so everybody goes one direction wrong or right but mostly wrong.

The Way forward

What you can confront, stay and deal with it but what you cannot confront, flee from it. In essence, you should flee from the crowd anytime you cannot confront it or else you would make the worst decisions of your life. When you are alone, you have all the space needed to think. The crowd easily read literal meaning to sentence but most of the time, we actually meant something else. Your spouse could just say that he or she hates you simply because you didn't do one particular thing he or she wanted you to do but that doesn't mean that he or she truly hates you. The literal meaning says he or she hates you but the emotional content is saying that he or she is angry over what you did.

Ask Advice from One Individual at a Time

There is nothing wrong with consulting members of friends and family but you should do that with a member at a time. One person at a time is less biased than two or more people at a time.

Women, most especially makes this mistake a lot. When they have more than one man asking them out, sometimes they get so indecisive on the one to accept. So they would bring the matter to the committee of friends. There is nothing wrong with discussing your issues with your friends and asking them for good advice but what I am telling you, is that you shouldn't make it a public show; try as much as possible to ask your friends individually at different times so you can be able to get a sincere response.

You would get a better result or advice when you consult people one at a time personally.

Wise Managing Directors, after calling for a meeting and giving everyone the free will to raise suggestions, still call back another or more members of staff to be interviewed one by one, personally, to get that concrete ideas or opinions about some specific issues affecting the organization.

The world had produced many great men and women and more are still being produced, but one common characteristic is that the great decisions that were made were personally made. The steps that were taken by them were mostly done individually until the rest of the world believed and followed them.

To be a success, you must learn how to always withdraw to yourself alone and make your final conclusion on key issues affecting you.

CHAPTER 59

Be Grateful For Your Yesterday, Today and the Future.

An average successful man is a grateful man. Stay close to him and you will find out that he is grateful for so many things. His tongue sing more praises than abuses. This is not to say that he doesn't have issues to worry about or people do not offend him, but he looks beyond his ugly pictures and concentrate more on the beautiful ones. Actually the beautiful pictures we have are usually more than the ugly pictures but most people spends more time staring at their ugly pictures and with time, that's all that they see and they end up even losing the beautiful ones yet to have.

Life is how you see it or Take it.
A happy people are happy not because they do not have problems but because they are still able to be happy even in the midst of their problems.

A king once promised that the entire artists in his city should come up with a very beautiful and sensible portrait, he gave them a dead line and the chosen one is to be handsomely rewarded. So all the artists went back to their studio and began to paint their very best.

All their portraits were submitted and the short listing began. At the end, two very best portraits were picked and the king had to make only one choice. The king looked at the first one; the city, mountains and everything surrounding it were so peaceful and beautiful. Then he picked the second portrait, inside the city was so calm and peaceful but it is being surrounded with war. The king fell in love with the second portrait and chose it. The king chose it because it was more realistic. The portrait portrayed a city that was peaceful even when they have a lot of troubles around them. In the real world, we need to always be happy because if we search very well, there is always a reason to be happy.

The point is that, to some extent, you are responsible for the kinds of life you live. If you want to live a successful and fulfilled life, then you need to change some of your actions. You need to change some of your patterns of living. You need to decide how you want to live and follow the rules that can take you there.

A lot of successful people see life as something beautiful not because they are successful. It is about their attitude towards life even before they became successful. They have always seen the good and the bad that happens as things that are working out for the best so whether a situation was favorable to them or not, they are happy.

The Power of Being Grateful.
Being grateful gives the power to achieve more. Being grateful even in an unfavorable condition gives victory in the long run.

There are people who drive better cars now because when their first car was stolen, they were still grateful to God and other things that they have.

Most wealthy people today had lost before to the point of almost giving up but their all-time grateful spirit somehow charged them up and they are able to come up again. Being grateful has a way of making you get more. I cannot really say how but I know it is good to have a grateful spirit.

Some ministries are bigger today because they stole from them a lot at their early stage but still maintained their gratefulness to God and the things they still have or would have.

Anytime I am being stolen from or cheated, I don't dwell so much on my loss and in no time I always get a better deal. Wrongs being done to you would pain you but don't let it get to your bones. Do you know whether something worse than that could have happened" so why let one incident take away your present blessings?

Always Look at the Brighter Side of Situations.
After merits and demerits, there is nothing else. All situations that have merits would also have demerits and nothing else. Life situation are two faced. the losers loose because they only see the demerit and the successful are successful because after seeing the demerits, they turn the page to the merits and they remain there.

CHAPTER 60

Make Your Expectations Moderate.

In your journey towards achievements, the road can never be smooth. It is full of obstacles. Both the ones you will bring upon yourself, others bring upon you and the ones nature will naturally test you with. The journey is full of so many heart breaks. Many a time you would have to pick up the pieces of your broken heart and move on.

Expect the Journey to Be Tough

When you expect something to be hard or tough, some cells are automatically activated in your body to prepare for the challenge. Psychological and mentally you become prepared and the chances of you winning increases.

For instance, when students prepare very well for a particular course, thinking that it is going to be difficult and when they finally wrote the exam on that particular course, it was simpler than they expected, there is this type of mood of joy the students will usually find themselves but the reason is because they expected it to be hard and so they prepared hard. The equation was balanced but do you know that there would also be some student from these same class that will complain that the course was tough because probably, they expected the examination for the course to be simpler or they didn't just give it a balancing preparation.

When You Are the One Giving, Make Your Expectations High

Each time you are the one to give out, make yourself high expectations. The reason being that: at worst, your output would still be able to stand you out. If you expect a job to be simpler and you prepare little for it and then it turns out to be tough, you would see yourself very far from your target and that psychologically put you down for a while when you need to be moving. Remember: no slowing down.

When you give a job very serious preparation and then it turns out to be simple for you and you accomplish your target, the joy is yours. The success is yours. In fact you lose nothing when you prepare very well.

During my graduation class in primary school, my class teacher gave us a slogan for us all in the graduating set to adopt. The slogan was "anything that is worth doing must be done well". With this new slogan, our method of doing things changed immediately. The competition in class became more competitive and those of us who were toping in academic and other areas started to work harder. Our class teacher made us understand that each time we do something; we must always give our best. He further went on to make us understand that it is better not to start at all than to do a poor job as long as it is something that is worth doing. Today when I look back and I remember all that, I always pray for him any where he is. He was able to raise our expectation and our performance got even better.

When You Are the One Receiving, Make Your Expectation Low

When you are the one receiving, you should make your expectation low because you are not in control of the output, you are not the one doing that work. The output would not be based on your own capacity but someone else own.

As we all know there is no journey to success that is one hundred percent (100%) smooth but if there are some rough edges you can remove yourself, why not do it? The reason why our heart breaks all the time is because we expect too much from others. You are the only type in the world. No any other is like you. When we set a standard for others based on our self, the result doesn't come out as expected and we get disappointed.

The only insurance on heartbreak is not expecting so much from others so when they perform below a certain level, you would not really feel bad or when you expect little and eventually you are giving more, your joy becomes times two (x2).

CHAPTER 61

Your Decisions of Yesterday Made Your Today And Your Decisions Of Today Would Make Your Tomorrow.

We are where we are today as a result of the various decisions we made in the past. Life is beautiful to the extent that it always presents us with choices to make. When people make bad mistakes and then they come out to say that they were left with no choice, it makes me upset because that's a lie. Let's take for instance, people who steal other people's properties decided to steal but when they get caught, majority claims they are poor and that they had no choice. The problem here is not really poverty but lack of integrity because there are people who are in that similar predicament and they never stole.

Everyone has dreams
Everyone has dreams but not everyone would live their dreams in the reality. The single factor that is responsible for this difference is our decisions.

One step is to dream, another is to follow it up with the right decisions. Out of a hundred people who wishes or dreams to achieve a goal, it is only one quarter that makes the right decisions and which normally achieve the goal. Sometimes the number could be less than one-quarter.

Obstacles Are Everywhere
Yes we know obstacles are everywhere but that is not really the reason why people fail to achieve their dreams.

The question is: when you were being thrown bricks at, what did you build with the bricks? Remember, it is only a fruitful tree that people throw stones at. But does that stop the tree from producing even more fruits every season? One other thing you should know is that, if you don't have obstacles, then you don't really have a dream. It is like the man whom people throw stones and bricks at; and then uses them to build what he had in mind. If he weren't thrown the stones and the bricks, what would he have built with? He could have as well done nothing about the stones and bricks being thrown at him. But it was his decision to build with them. As a matter of fact, his decision made him.

Think Carefully Before Making Decisions
The most regretted decisions were the ones made in haste without thinking carefully. Life is like a moving locomotive, it doesn't have a reverse so you should think carefully because you can't turn back the hands of time. Take your time to carefully decide your destination before jumping into that train.

All decisions do not have the same amount of importance. Some are more important than the others and they are made maybe once in a lifetime, such decisions deserve deep consultation before finally being made. Every human being has such type of decisions. For instance, the decision of your life career path is an important one and it cannot be decided in a day. It will even affect the type of friends you should keep, the type of brother or sister you should be and so on.

Some people are doomed for life because they followed their friends to do sciences when they are naturally good in creative art or the other way round. They were disciples for too long that they can't even come back anymore. All this boils down to bad decisions made yesterday and they affect our today negatively. Good decisions of yesterday also affects our today positively.

With all the natural endowment of some countries, they are still poor and under developed because of the bad decisions which were made by its leaders. Some countries are coming up fast because their leaders have decided to implement good decisions.

You should be able to know from among the options, which one will be more favorable to you not in the short time but in the long run. Decision always goes with action. If you decide without any action, you have made no decision.

Your Chance to Make a Better Tomorrow
For the fact that you live today, it is a chance for you to make tomorrow better. Nothing is too late to do especially when it has to do with someone's happiness. I don't want to know if your yesterday was great or not, what matter now is what you are doing with the air you are breathing now. Besides it is better to end well than start well and end miserably.

Some made the right decisions yesterday and it gave them positive result and so when it got to today, they relaxed, their future would be full of regrets. I hate it when people discuss the good old days because today is supposed to be better than yesterday and tomorrow, better than today. No matter the mistakes you have made yesterday due to bad decisions, as long as you breath today, that is a chance to make your tomorrow better.

CHAPTER 62

No Trumpet Sound When the Important Decision of Our Life Are Made. Destiny Is Made Known Silently.

One secret to being successful is maintaining some level of secrecy. It isn't every time you would let people know what you are up to. Already every goal has enough obstacles so do everything to avoid extra or unnecessary rough stones and one way of getting this done is by maintaining some levels of secrecy. The following are some of the harmful implications associated with announcing to the world your intentions.

Exposure to Public Eye
When too many people start to know about your intentions, your goals and plans stand a higher risk of not being able to be achieved because most of these people you have told have nothing positive to contribute but rather limit your chances of achievement.

Human beings have a way of developing a secret envy especially when the other person is becoming more successful, true friends and supporters are hard to come by but enemies who pretend to be friends are everywhere. Making your goals or your plans known to everyone would only increase the number of your enemies which is not good for you.

High Expectation from People

Every time you discuss your beautiful dreams with people or tell whoever cares to listen about your great plans, you raise people's expectation for you and if you ended not performing up to their expectation, they would be disappointed in you. Most great achievements came to many people as surprise. Not even all family members usually know. Another thing is that when you spend so much energy telling the world about your dreams, you won't really have much energy to focus and plan actions that would help you in achieving your dreams.

You do not need to announce success. Success has a way of announcing itself. As a matter of fact success can't be hidden. Work in secret as much as possible, your success would later announce itself. In a situation where by you didn't run your mouth, your success will take people by surprise and they will be impressed no matter how small your success may be. But when you run your mouth, everybody would be looking forward to what you will do. Eventually you achieve a success that is not up to their expectation; you would be seen as an empty drum, making the loudest noise.

Involve Only Those Who Has Positive Contribution

There is a saying that: too many cooks spoil the food. When you draft goals to be achieved, it is like someone who has decided to cook. The same thing goes to the man who has a goal or dream to achieve.

It is certain that very few people always have something positive to contribute to our life. This is more reason why we need to source out for the positive contributors carefully. Human beings were not created in isolation and so every plan or goal always have stakeholders. The qualification and dedication of the stakeholders always determine the level of success to be achieved.

Contribution (positive) can be in so many ways and are as follow:
- Financial,
- Moral,
- Words of encouragement,
- Advice,
- Time dedication and so much more.

You need to know the various areas where your friends and family members are talented so you can know who to meet for particular issues.

The World Do Not Care Until You Make It

Actually, the world doesn't care until you make it. What you intend to do and how to go about it is your own headache, the world don't care. So why waste your energy announcing your goals, dreams or plans. What the world need you to do is to adopt the particular behavioral pattern that will yield you positive results.

CHAPTER 63

Everybody Has Their Own Definition of Success but One Thing Is Sure: Success Is A Positive Growth In Any Aspect Of Our Lives

We have at one time or the other achieved success in a particular thing that we set out to accomplish. One way or the other, we have all had moments of success because success is that thing you set out to achieve and which eventually you did.

Some people are referred to as being successful not because they have achieved everything they set out to achieve or would achieve everything they set out to achieve but because they have been able to achieve a tremendous success in one or more aspect of their lives which also served as blessing to others.

If you had planned to visit three of your colleagues in a particular Saturday and eventually, you were able to achieve that. That is success but success from only your personal point of view. For you to be seen as a successful man from majority point of view, your success must carry a heavy weight. It must be obvious enough for everyone to see. Majority should be able to testify that you are doing well.

A Real success must be able to touch enough aspects of your life.
Some people are called poor while others are called, rich not

because those that are called poor don't really have money but they have very little degree of money. In our own little ways, we have achieved success in one area or the other of our life but you need a tremendous success that is capable of putting you in the spot light for the whole world to see that you are successful.

You need a success that will touch enough aspects of your life for you to be called successful. Life has so many segments, become an authority in one. If you want to be a doctor, be a top doctor, if it is to be a barrister, become a top barrister, if it is music you want to do, become a top musician. The backseat is not for you. Any segment or aspect you have chosen to dwell in, become an authority there.

As you become an authority in a particular area, the benefits you will get shall cover for your inadequacy in other areas and yet, the world would still see you as a successful person.

A tremendous success in a particular aspect also has a way of bringing out other talents you have. For instance, there are well known musicians who later embraced the movie industry. Their first love which was music created the platform. A tremendous success in one area is capable of touching or changing your lifestyle completely. That is what they call real success. Endeavour to achieve that.

Find Out Your Natural Strengths
Find out your natural strengths, it would be easier for you to become an authority there with much training. There are areas God has blessed every one of us with. With little trial, we become successful in such areas which mean that with more dedication and focus, you can become an authority.

CHAPTER 64

The Road To Success Is Full Of Stress So If You Must Succeed, You Must Learn How To Manage Stress.

Stress is part of our everyday living. As we go about our daily routine, stress is one thing that goes along with it. And if not managed properly, it is capable of destroying you. Since stress is something that we cannot take out of our life, the only way is for us to manage it properly.

There is a saying that: who has health, has wealth. This is because he, who is healthy, can be able to create further wealth. Even as you want to achieve the whole world in a day, watch the signs because it is only when you are healthy that you can be able to carry on. As a healthy man, you have more chances of being successful.

Possible Symptoms of Stress
The symptoms are categorized into mental and physical.

Mental symptoms
➤ Depression
➤ Feeling tired
➤ Angry
➤ Not being able to sleep
➤ Not being able to focus.

Physical Symptoms
> Chest pains
> Loss of appetite
> Muscle aches
> Diarrhea
> Feeling restless

Above are just some few possible symptoms of stress. When you are going through any of the above symptoms, it is advisable to see the doctor for further consultation.

Ways to Manage Stress

Exercise Regularly
Aerobic exercise is said to release endorphins that help you in feeling better and at the same time maintaining positive attitude. Exercise would help you to sweat and break the stress that must have been building up in you.

Maintain a Balance diet
You need to eat right and drink right. When food and drinks are not taken sensibly, it is capable of causing more stress to you.

Adopt relaxation techniques
Put it as part of your time table to always relax. There must be something that put that smile on your face such as sporting activities where you can engage in friendly matches, a good time out with the family etc.

Reduce stressors
Life, most times has too many demands and you still have the normal 24hrs per day that everyone is having. What you need to do is to select the ones you can handle for the day, and then

push the rest forward. Screen the demands on you. So you can see yourself attending to only the important ones.

Above are ways to manage stress. But there are more. You can meet your doctor or simply goggle it out and you will be surprised at the numerous activities that will be exposed to you.

CHAPTER 65

Life And Death Is In The Tongue, Be Careful Of The One You Let Out.

Words are powerful. They can make you and at the same time, break you. Out of the abundance of the mind, the mouth speaketh. This is more reason why you need to always be in control of your mind set. Keep your mind positive always and it will reflect in your tongue and would further pass into your actions.

I feel that nature is a being and she is a witness to everything we do including what our tongue confesses. Her ears and eyes are always opened and anytime she hears us, she takes note. Usher mom once advised him: son, be careful of what you wish for because you might just get it. You know it happens. Especially the ones that is bad. It seems as if the moment you wished, some beings were waiting to process your wish. Maybe we have more bad spirits than the good ones after all; we have more bad people than the good ones. So anytime you make a negative wish, there are more hands processing it to come true and that's why bad things happen fast.

On the other hand, it seems as though when you wish for something good or pray for something good, the bad spirits will start trying to prevent the good spirits from processing it. Although it would still come through but it takes longer. You know definitely, the bad spirits would be more violent and forceful in their action than the good spirits.

Another thing I feel is that there is a court in heaven, the moment you pray to God for something and He is about to grant your request, the Satan shows up and start giving all the reasons in the world why you do not deserve what you asked for. Maybe that explains the reason why some prayers take long to be answered.

Be positive in mind always

They say the spiritual control the physical and to a great extent, it is true. At least it explains the reason why people go into the state of coma and then come back to life. Physically they were dead but because their spirit didn't die, the body was forced to accept life again. All the run around from one place to another, the organizing, directing, and controlling just to make a particular plan work are the physical part of being successful. Actually the cement that glues the bridge together is the positive spirit that the plan can be achieved. It is that positive spirit that the goal can be achieved that actually motivated all the other physical activities. All gears towards being successful.

It is normal to be offended and then you get angry but do not let anger gets to your mind. When people offend you, forgive those that trespass against you, you are doing yourself a favor because it keeps your mind more balanced and positive. A balanced and positive mind is more capable of making good decisions and whether you and I like it or not, the improvement on mankind we enjoy today is as a result of good decisions.

Still Speak Life Even When the Cloud Is Darkest

Success is not external alone, it comes from the internal as well as life. People may be looking healthy but if well examined, they are not. A dark cloud is like an external show. It doesn't really have the power to influence the real situation. Speak life even when the cloud is darkest, as long as you have life, in no time, the dark cloud shall give its way for a silver lining in the sky. There had been situations where by someone is admitted in the hospital and physically by real calculation; he has no chance of making it back to life but the patient kept hoping and speaking life and eventually, he was restored back to life in good health.

The successful business moguls you hear of today are the ones that refuse to give up even when the cloud is darkest. I know of a movie I watched many years ago. The title is: never back down. The actor was a ring fighter and many times he was almost beaten to death but he preferred to rather die than live as a defeat and somehow he became champion in the fight.

It All Starts With the Tongue
Life and death both starts with the tongue. Sorcerers make their incantations through their tongue. Jesus Christ healed many by speaking just as the world was created by God with words. So there is really power in the tongue.

Martin-Luther king used words to communicate his American dream and that positive spirit he displayed through his tongue still made positive changes to take place even after this death. One single word of discouragement before his death would have led to the end of his American dream but he never gave that chance even when the cloud was darkest.

Your Word Is the Water Used For Watering the Seed
All your efforts towards being successful and great can be likened to that of a farmer sowing his seeds. The positive words you speak serve as the water that waters the farmer's seeds. If the farmer uses water to water his seeds, it is because he knows the benefits of watering his plants and so he takes his time to get good water that is free from contamination to water his seeds.

CHAPTER 66

We Have Dreams and Destiny But Our Destiny Supersedes Our Dreams

Life is like a movie and we are the casts. Some are to act as the prince or members of the royal families, others as servants of the kingdom. We can be rest assured that if we are all given a choice to pick the role we would like to act, nobody would take the script of a servant. Destiny explains the reason why you are born with a silver spoon and others, with a golden spoon; some were even born spoonless. If you had been given the opportunity, you would have probably abandoned your silver spoon for a golden one.

Thank God for Dreams

I say thank God for dreams because it gives us the hope that we can change our situation. Take for instance, a palace maid becoming the palace Queen if she gets married to the king or the crowned prince who later ascend to the throne of the king. I believe dreams come true. Yea, dreams do come true but not all dreams come true. A dream well chased after has more chances of coming true. The good thing about dreams is that it gives you the belief that your tomorrow shall be like how you want it to be. Maybe you are poor now, dream would give you the hope that you will be rich tomorrow and with that, you won't give much attention to your current predicament just because all that your eyes sees is the brighter tomorrow and that makes you happy already.

Our dreams are always in accordance with our desires. Like I said earlier on, some do come true but even if some don't come true, but the hope they must have given to you is a benefit because they gave you a reason to live on. If man is sure that his tomorrow won't be anything better, he would rather commit suicide now than live on. But dreams provide the hope for a better tomorrow and that is what keeps us moving.

Our Destiny Supersedes Our Dreams

When people put their best into something and at the end, they see a disappointing result, some would say: what would be would be. This is just simply saying that destiny shall prevail.

You may fight to get something now and you end up losing it, then later in the future, destiny let you have it. It becomes a thing of joy. But at the same time, if it weren't your destiny to have it, it would have been gone forever.

Destiny is capable of crashing your dreams. It is not everything you should dream to have or fight to have because no matter how much you follow up, you would never get it.

Build Your Dreams around Your Destiny

Every one of us has a destiny to fulfill. That destiny we have to fulfill is the reason why God still over look our wrong doings. At the first place, our destiny is the purpose why we came to earth. Our being on earth has a master plan. The master plan is not known to us. We are made to forget everything the moment we are born but to make the movie more interesting, we just keep on acting according to the script not knowing which one is next we are to act.

If your movie script says you are the king or the Queen, your dreams should centre on that as well or else at the appropriate time, destiny would still prevail and it will now, look like as if life is unfair. Save yourself those tears by building your dreams around your destiny but first, you must have an idea of your destiny.

Knowing Your Destiny
Take your time and begin to remember all the things you derives passion in doing; most especially, the ones that came to you naturally. In school there were those courses that we didn't study so hard and yet we made the best grade in them.

Pay a visit to an authority, it could be your spiritual leader, a counselor in that field etc. you may not get exactly what you are looking for but it would help you have an idea of what your destiny look like so that you can build your dreams around it.

Name Index

A
Alicia Keys, 157
Aristotle (384-322BC), 19
Arthur Rubinstein, 181

B
Barrack Obama, 9, 10, 21, 59, 139, 151
Ben Carson, 24
Benjamin Disreali (1804-81), 11
Bob Gass, 67, 68

C
Charles Babage, 59

D
Dandison, 123
David, 12, 17, 172

E
Edward Hillary, 58
Euripides, 183

H
Hoan Logic Baild, 59

J
Jay-Z, 25
John Buroughs, 149, 150
John Mason, 57, 60, 63, 83, 158
Johnann Gutenbery, 59

Joseph, 91, 92

L
Lionel Messi, 157

M
Mariah Carey, 118, 157
Maxwell Mattz, 29
Michael Jackson, 14, 57, 157
Michael Jordan, 17, 68

N
Nelson Mandela, 6, 62

O
Old Epitaph, 153
Orison Marden, 157
Orville, 59
Oxford Advance Learner Dictionary, 9

R
Rev. Canon Saturday T. Nbete, 171

S
Samuel Glover, 145
Solomon, 12, 15, 16, 172
Solomon Gabriel, 15

T
The Midrash (AD 400-500), 3
Theodore Roethke, 9
Tony Robins, 25

W
William Fox Taibo, 59
Wright, 59

Z
Zacchaeus, 12
Zuckerberg, 110

Subject Index

A

Action, 2, 25, 43, 45, 54, 100, 201
Advantage, 37

B

Being brave, 37
Being Physically Strong, 37
Betrayal, 115
Boldness, 201
Bricks, 63, 64, 66, 111, 220
Business enterprises, 22, 142

C

Calculated risk, 29, 31, 85, 86, 121
Childhood Hobbies, 159
Comfort zones, 110
Communication, 71
Competence, 89
confidential person, 13
Conscious, 11
consistency, 104, 105
Consistency, 88, 104, 150

D

Disappointment, 114

E

Electric bulb, 59
Entertainment industry, 22, 34
Everlasting Joy, 128
Extrovert, 13

F

Facebook, 110

Famous, 23, 33, 57, 166
Forgiveness, 80, 179

G

Grace, 171, 172, 173
Greatness, 1, 2

H

Hard work, 1, 22, 67, 123, 173
Highly reserved person, 14
Humility, 170, 190

I

Ignorance, 11
Information warehouse, 16
Interest at heart, 97
Interrelatedness, 169
Introvert, 14

L

Lack of Discipline, 150

M

Memory, 15, 16, 18
Microsoft Mission, 142
Microsoft Vision, 142
Mission, 141
Mother and child relationship, 97
Mount Everest, 58

N

Natural Laws, 100

P

Paparazzi, 24
Penetrate, 13
Poor man, 33, 71, 72, 73
Power/influence, 37
Practice, 15
Practice makes perfect, 6, 17, 24
Procrastination, 28, 149
Purpose, 5, 6, 42, 44

R

Real Decision, 25
Reasonable decisions, 15
Regret, 114
Revenge, 79
Rich man, 33, 71, 72, 73, 165
Right attitude, 66, 110, 147, 182
Rome was not built in a day, 22
Rules, 1

S

Save, 93, 133, 145, 238
School System, 119
Secret Enemies, 176
Selfishness, 55
Selflessness, 56
Sensational singer, 23
Short time Joy, 129
Silence, 15, 18, 135, 136
Smartness, 76
storing information, 16
strength, 6, 37, 38, 39, 64, 84, 99, 109, 118
Stress, 229, 230
Success, 1, 24, 31, 32, 69, 97, 110, 123, 124, 138, 139, 146, 147, 157, 175, 184, 186, 204, 216, 217, 224, 227, 228
Success, 147, 184, 202, 224, 227, 229, 234
Successful, 23, 48, 54, 64, 86, 142, 158, 161, 162, 167, 175, 181, 182, 190, 200, 211, 212, 213, 223, 227, 228, 235
Successful man, 162, 175, 211, 227

T

Talent, 5, 6, 42, 83, 84, 95, 96, 97, 169
Teaching Others, 15
The Ability, 37, 117, 119
Till Day Break, 123
Time, 2, 121, 141, 145, 200, 208, 225
Titanic Ship, 124
Trespassing, 178
Trust, 135, 136
TV personalities, 14

U

Unforeseen circumstance, 120
United Nations Organization, 39
Unity, 38, 39, 40
University system, 22
Unmerited Favor, 172
UNO, 39

V

Vision, 91, 141, 142
Vision Extinguisher, 91
Vision Molders, 91

W

Will Power, 87
Wisdom, 15

For Booking

E.J. Ipheghe customizes his speech for different audiences such as Business seminars, Talks on career, motivation etc

You can contact him by sending a message to jayworld00@yahoo.com

www.ingramcontent.com/pod-product-compliance
Lightning Source LLC
Chambersburg PA
CBHW051647040426
42446CB00009B/1020